The Winning Mind

Fernhurst Books

The Winning Mind

John Whitmore

First published 1987 by
Fernhurst Books, 53 High Street, Steyning, West Sussex BN4 3LA

Printed and Bound in Great Britain.

ISBN 0 906754 30 5

Photographic credits

Tim Hore: pages 6, 23, 27, 30, 32, 34, 49, 52, 63
Kos: page 40
Yachting Photographics: cover, pages 2-3, 10, 15, 39, 45, 55
Gary Burke: page 8

Acknowledgements

Thanks first and foremost to Tim Gallwey who taught me the
Inner Game which forms the basis of my perspective on sports
psychology. Secondly I am especially grateful to Tim Davison
for having the courage to ask me to write this book and the
patience to put hours of discussion onto paper in a form from
which I could work. Thirdly I thank the following sailors:
Tony Morgan, Ed Baird, Eric Twiname, Paul Elvstrom, Rodney
Pattisson and Lawrie Smith, who provided anecdotes and
experiences upon which I drew for examples.

John Whitmore

Design by John Woodward
Composition by A&G Photoypesetters, Knaphill, Surrey
Printed by Ebenezer Baylis & Son Ltd, Worcester

Contents

Foreword

John Whitmore once joined me on a business trip to Australia in the late 1960s, and on a day of leisure I took him sailing aboard *Gretel II*, on a training trip with Jim Hardy who was sharpening up for the America's Cup.

After hours of intense effort off the Heads in light breezes, with twelve men or more rushing about from tack to tack, Hardy eventually inquired of John 'Enjoying the sport?' John Whitmore, a recently retired racing driver accustomed to speeds of up to 200 m.p.h., suggested that 'It is an awful lot of rushing about to achieve a little less than walking speed'.

What a delight therefore to find that John, some twenty years later, has acquired sufficient affection for sailing and sailors to write such an effective work. He shows a remarkable understanding of the problems that sailors are regularly faced with – problems that, more often than not, originate within the sailors' own minds. *The Winning Mind* is about sharing the secret of how to win, something I personally feel to be as satisfying as winning itself.

John Whitmore's insights into the psychology of successful sailing could be applied to any sport, or for that matter to the greater competition of life itself. It is a book that doesn't have to be confined to the shelf marked 'Sailing' – though that's as good a place as any to start from . . .

Tony Morgan
Silver Medal, Flying Dutchman
Olympic Games (Tokyo).
Owner *More Opposition*
Class 1 Admiral's Cup Team
(Switzerland)

There is only one winner
And if you compete at high enough levels
You know it's not going to be you.

BUT YOU TRY!
The challenge is in the trying,
The fun lives in the trying.

If you give one hundred per cent
Don't make any mistakes
And still get beat,

If you come back to the beach completely
exhausted
But with clear eyes, and all the cobwebs
blown out,

Hell man, you just won!

Jack Sammons
Welcome to A Fleet

1 Mind matters

Only your mind stands between you and the sailing championship you covet. It has the potential to make you a champion – but it can also make a pretty good job of sabotaging your efforts. You may spend a stack of money on your boat, read every book on tactics which you can lay your hands on, and develop your sailing technique to a high standard, but all will be of no avail if you do not also learn to master your own mind.

You know the feeling. It's blowing Force 6 and you're streaking towards the gybe mark. You're doing pretty well and know you have a good chance of winning if only you can stay upright. And then the rot sets in.

'Now come on, be positive' says the little voice in your head. 'Take the sheet straight from the boom, get the tiller extension out to leeward. Make sure you're travelling at full speed down a wave before you gybe. Oh no, that gust's going to hit just at the crucial moment. Oh well, here goes. You idiot, *duck* when the boom comes over. Now straighten up – not too much. You're crazy, the boat's rolling on top of you. Don't let out the sheet. . .'

And so it goes on. From your position on the upturned hull you watch the champion sail by, gybe effortlessly and hammer off down the reach. 'I told you so', says the little voice.

Californian tennis coach Tim Gallway put it very well in his best-selling book *The Inner Game of Tennis* when he wrote that the opponent in your own head is often more daunting than the one on the other side of the net – or, we might add, in the other boat. The secret of beating that opponent is to understand something about how your mind works: how it helps you and how it sabotages you, and how to acquire some practical means of adjusting its effects to your advantage.

The anxious mind

Several years ago a *Sports Illustrated* survey placed sailing and motor sport at the top of the list of sports demanding a developed intellect. The complexity of these two activities, the sophisticated equipment involved and the variability of the conditions in which it has to operate, make the qualities of knowledge, analysis and logic essential to success.

We are all familiar with these intellectual qualities, even if, as individuals, we vary in our ability to deploy them. Equally familiar however are a number of other mental effects which are not so welcome, such as frustration, bravado and timidity, and it is these which form the opponent in your own head. The common factor which links them all is anxiety, or more specifically, self-doubt.

Different sports vary widely in the scope they provide for anxiety. Golf, for example, provides plenty of opportunities for anxiety during the game: it is repeatedly rebuilt between shots. By contrast, downhill ski racing involves very high risks, with the result that the potential for pre-race anxiety is enormous, but the build-up of nervous tension is swept away in the instant of the start and has no opportunity to return in the subsequent rush. In sailing there is some risk to the crew and the boat – furthermore there is often ample time to think about it, particularly in offshore racing. Even when the real risks are slight, anxiety about tactics or tuning can often build up during the intervals between complex, mentally demanding manoeuvres.

This anxiety is not always experienced as simple nail-biting worry. It is often disguised as a sensible evaluation of options, or an effort to apply someone else's theory. We might call this whole area of mental activity the anxious mind. It chatters, instructs, criticizes, warns and generally interferes with us much of the time. It usually leads us right into the many pitfalls that it claims to be trying to help us to avoid – and then it says 'I told you so!' Although this saboteur, this anxious mind, will protest that it is utterly rational and logical, it is the product, and to some extent, the cause of our own self-

doubt. The result is that in sport, as in life, we tend to be tossed around by the waves of our desires and emotions.

The natural mind

Although we are sometimes overwhelmed by the frenzied activity of the anxious mind, there is a natural, healthy and efficient part of the mind which will function very well by itself with the minimum of fuss – if we allow it to. We are all familiar with the experience, not as frequent as we would like perhaps, of doing something in a fluid, economical and efficient way which seems to take almost no effort. This often happens while the anxious mind is otherwise engaged. You may be worrying about financial problems while walking home; before you know it

Below: Don't let anxiety or self-doubt sabotage your efforts.

you are at your gate, having safely negotiated all obstacles, crossed several roads, and followed a complex route through a network of city streets. With no direction from your anxious mind, your natural mind has taken charge and quietly and efficiently delivered you to your door. Animals, wild ones at least, are like this most of the time. When a falcon dives out of the sky onto its victim it does not calculate its velocity and trajectory – if it did it would probably miss. Similarly a touch-typist does not stop to think where the letters are; she has to trust her natural mind to find the right keys while her intellect is engaged in finding the right words.

To be like this – to function fluidly, economically and efficiently we need to calm the anxious mind and trust the natural mind. Only then will we be able to co-ordinate the many parts of ourselves – along with our crew and our boat – in the way a conductor takes charge of the orchestra when he taps his baton to still the cacophany of tuning instruments.

Ways and means

So much for the strategy, but what of the tactics? How do you liberate the natural mind from its overburden of misapplied intellect and anxiety?

The first step is to isolate a few mental qualities such as self-confidence which are unrelated to intellectual achievement, yet invaluable in any situation. You might like to list a few such qualities – which you as a sailor consider valuable – in the grey box below. Remember we are looking now at 'inner' qualities like self-confidence rather than acquired 'outer' qualities like experience or skill.

Now look at my list on the next page. Opposite each basic quality I have added some other words that do not necessarily mean the same thing, but are related to

Inner qualities

Inner qualities

Responsibility	Humility
Awareness	Sensitivity, Observation, Clarity
Concentration	Focused attention
Relaxation	Calmness, Flow
Detachment	Calmness, Observation
Commitment	Motivation, Tenacity, Intention, Will
Trust	Self-confidence, Courage

them or stem from them. The list is by no means exhaustive and I have deliberately omitted those qualities so essential for membership of a team or a crew as this subject is fully dealt with in a later chapter.

Take a careful look at the qualities on both your list and mine, and rate yourself on a 1-5 scale. If you generate 100 per cent commitment every time you sail, give yourself 5 on that one, and so on.

You now have some idea of the way you would *like* to be when you are sailing, and your ratings give you a measure of the way you usually are. The next chapter will elaborate on the qualities on my list, and throughout the book you will find more ways in which you can build upon your positive qualities, suppress the chattering of the anxious mind and encourage the natural, clean efficiency that will make you a winner.

2 Essential mental qualities

Responsibility, detachment, awareness, concentration... familiar enough as words, but what do we mean by them? A thorough understanding of these qualities is basic to the whole concept of the winning mind.

Responsibility

The principle of responsibility is very hard to embrace fully. How often do we hear sailors excuse their poor performance by saying 'If only the weather had been different/one of my crew had not been sick/I had got a better start/a better boat/a better sail' etc? Such people will never win until they take responsibility for their successes and failures. That may include doing whatever it takes to get a better start, boat or sail.

A good way to begin is to verbalise things differently. For example, 'if only the weather had been different', could be expressed as 'I am less skilled in such and such a type of weather' or, 'I failed to anticipate the change in the weather'.

Weather is just weather, it is not good or bad, it is just the way it is – and it probably doesn't care what you think of it either. External circumstances such as weather, the boat, or being a crew member short are generally less of a problem than how we react to them internally. For every change in situation we have an inner response, and while the situation is often beyond our control, our response to it is not. We empower ourselves by taking responsibility instead of blaming the situation. By describing rather than decrying it, we define an area to act upon now or to learn more about later. We can welcome challenges or allow ourselves to be beset with problems. The choice is ours.

Awareness

This brings us to the second principle, awareness. Awareness is our experience of what is going on here and now. It is not our ideas, judgements, opinions, analyses, fears, criticism, complaints and thoughts about what is going on. Experience, as I am using it here, is something that comes to us through our senses, not through our minds. For you it may be the feeling of the tiller in your hand, the wind on your face or the tightness of your muscles. It may be the slapping of the hull on the water or the flapping of the sails in the breeze. It may be just observing your thoughts, concerns, fears or expectations as they flutter through your mind. Awareness is what you have to sharpen to find the response to the questions, 'What is happening' and 'What am I doing?'

If we are not aware of what is going on or what we are doing, how can we respond effectively? Awareness empowers us to take responsibility. 'Of course I am always aware? you may snort. Yes, you probably are, but there is an infinite depth to awareness and there is no-one who cannot go deeper and deeper into their experiencing, and reap the benefits of so doing. Awareness itself is curative, by which I mean that when an experience becomes conscious, self-correction often occurs at a subconscious level.

How many crew members suffer from aches and pains after a hard day's sailing which are the result of using their bodies inefficiently? If we experience what is going on in our bodies while we are performing some action our bodies will automatically make the fine adjustments necessary to do it more efficiently – adjustments too subtle for us to make by visual analysis or improvements in technique.

Awareness can be enhanced also by the simple device of substituting descriptive terms for judgemental ones. For example: 'My arm hurts' is not very helpful, but 'My wrist is twisted to the left and my lower arm muscle burns when I pull on the sheet' locates the problem, describes it and gives some idea of what to do about it.

The focusing of attention that is required to describe accurately the body sensation, the associated emotion or the associated thought will immediately start to dissolve it. Of course what we normally do is the opposite: we try to shut bad things out. That can be done too by substitution, as we shall see later, but as a general rule 'that which we resist persists'.

Concentration

Concentration is focused awareness. Contrary to what many people believe, it is a passive receptive state, to be compared with a camera with its lens directed at a particular spot. All too often it is confused with trying hard. At school I was frequently commanded to try harder – or to concentrate – and this produced in me quite the reverse effect, something akin to paranoia. If at first we don't succeed in an endeavour, we tend to try harder but this conscious effort rarely produces results. It merely impedes what natural facility we have. The greatest achievements in sport generally occur in a state best described as relaxed concentration.

Perhaps the clearest experience of true concentration that most of us have is while we are listening to a piece of music that we really enjoy. We place our attention upon the sound to the exclusion of all else and we ride with that sound without making any attempt to influence or interpret it. We simply experience it. This does not mean that the body has to be inactive at the same time. Many skiers have experienced their best ski run while concentrating exclusively on the stereo rock music from their personal tape players. Ever tried sailing with a Walkman?

Relaxation

Awareness and concentration occupy our minds fully and free us from the constant chatter of self-instruction and self-criticism that sportspeople so often subject themselves to. One effect of this is that the body, liberated from the barrage, is able to relax and get on with the job in hand.

Most people are fairly relaxed as they walk but just for a moment try giving yourself some walking instruction and criticising the result. Notice how awkward your walk becomes. Now cut the chatter and walk with your awareness focused either on the feeling in your whole body as you walk, or on the feeling in a particular part of your body, or on the normally unnoticed twittering of small birds in the vicinity. Notice how relaxed your walk feels now.

Detachment

Awareness requires some capacity for self-observation. We can divide ourselves into two parts, that which is having the experience and that which is noticing it. If, as I mentioned earlier, you are being tossed upon the waves of your emotions, you seem to become your emotions and they pervade you. If on the other hand you step back a little, you can watch yourself experiencing emotions. This process is sometimes described as detachment, disidentification or self-awareness. Recognising that you have emotions but you are not ruled by them is very liberating. It is only when you can find this liberated place within yourself that you can take the helm and steer yourself into calmer waters.

Commitment

A lot is made of the will to win in sport, and even the competitive world of business employs sporting metaphors such as target and goal. None of these words carry quite

Below: Relaxed concentration is the key to sporting efficiency.

as much relevance as the term commitment.

Commitment can be built in three steps. The first step is to ensure that the goal which you are to commit yourself to is realisable. If it is not, you must set a realisable intermediate goal. The second step is to systematically eliminate the external and internal obstacles to the achievement of that goal. The third step is to keep observing the level of commitment you are generating, both before and during a competition, and being honest with yourself about it. 100 per cent commitment to a realisable goal will invariably produce success, while 80 per cent commitment will equally certainly not. We will look in more detail at how commitment can be raised later in the book.

Trust

Finally some people, like my school teacher, advocate or demand a 'try harder' philosophy, and it works for some people. For others it introduces anxiety or rebellion which is counter-productive and may override all the beneficial effects of the increase in focus on the goal which the injunction also evokes. What we need to attain is goal clarity without the anxiety. This is why the concepts of commitment and trust are more effective than trying hard. Trust here means trusting yourself, trusting your mind and your body to reproduce the best of all they have learned and experienced as it is needed. It means trusting that with 100 per cent commitment and 100 per cent awareness, you will automatically and effortlessly give the best performance you are capable of, given your present level of skill and with the present equipment and conditions. If your sport involves using complex and sophisticated equipment, as sailing certainly does, then it means trusting that too. Ultimately it is trusting life, the Universe and God. . . but that is another story!

3 Internal obstacles

The opposite of trust is doubt, and self-doubt is the cause of most of the internal obstacles which prevent us achieving sporting excellence.

Internal obstacles are all those problems that reside within the boundary of our own skins. An obvious example is temporary or chronic tension in various parts of the body, from the easily recognised ache in the thighs and shoulders to more subtle tightness in the facial muscles or the scalp.

It is not difficult to understand how tension makes movements slow and mechanical, and destroys the natural flow so vital to top performers in every sport. Tension can be temporarily relieved using some forms of exercise or massage, but that is only treating the symptoms. It is working from the outside in, and we need to reach deeper to achieve a lasting effect. One way of working from the inside out is to use focused awareness or observation of the precise body sensations in the tense area. It often helps to deliberately increase the tension as much as possible, hold it for half a minute and then let go, all the while focusing your awareness on the area concerned.

Tension is only one of the ways our thoughts and our feelings have a direct and restricting effect on our physical actions. There are many such causes and effects and they differ widely from person to person. If you can, list the internal obstacles that you have encountered while sailing, using the grey box below.

Internal obstacles		
Major obstacles	**Recurring problems**	**Occasional irritations**

Now we have something to work on! Your list will almost certainly contain some of the following:

- Fear of injury, fear of failure or fear of ridicule
- Over-analysis, trying too hard, or obsession with technique.
- Self-instruction or self-criticism.
- Expectations of failure or aims that are too high
- Inability to relax, observe, detach or trust
- Avoidance of responsibility

All of these can be traced to self-doubt. Permanently eliminating long-term, ingrained self-doubt, and all its manifestations in one go is by no means easy, and it is the subject of the next chapter. However, short-term solutions can be quite effective during a competition, and if they are used regularly they do begin to have long-term effects.

There are some internal obstacles which do not arise from self-doubt. These include:

- Lack of motivation, loss of concentration or lack of clarity
- Laziness, boredom or tiredness
- Obstinacy, spite or aggression

If any of the problems I have mentioned apply to you, add them to your list if they are not already there.

Tackling the problem

The internal obstacles on these three lists (including your own) recur again and again in all sports. Sometimes they can be reduced or eliminated simply by increasing one's awareness of their existence as thoughts, emotions or body sensations. If you cannot identify a thought or isolate a feeling sufficiently to focus your awareness on it, then ask yourself the question, 'How do I know I am bored, afraid or tired?' The place to work on, be it in the body or the mind, will then reveal itself.

Behind every physical problem like tension there is an associated thought and an emotion. Conversely every thought will be reflected in a bodily response which we interpret as an emotion. Furthermore every emotion will evoke associated thoughts and bodily changes both in sensation and in posture. There is no beginning and no end to this cycle. One may enter it at any point. A person dominated by his or her mind will notice it first through a thought, while more emotionally orientated people will experience it first through a feeling or an emotion. Whichever is affected first, it is important to realise that all three are affected and that the problem can be tackled through the mind, the body or the emotions.

Self coaching

Usually, when attempting to overcome an internal obstacle, it is best to focus upon the most overt manifestation. This is likely to be the body sensation but it will depend on both the particular problem being tackled and the individual's make-up. Physically active people generally respond best to work on body sensations; some academics on the other hand would probably need to be approached through their minds to achieve the best response.

Let us use an example of a sailing situation to illustrate how a problem arises, and how self-coaching may be used.

The wind suddenly cuts up rough and an irregular wave catches you unawares, dumping a ton of water into the boat. The thought that you might capsize or sink which flashes through your mind is accompanied almost simultaneously by an overheating of your solar plexus, and you know you are afraid. The boat staggers but recovers and the thought subsides; the

What? When? Where? How much?

Ask yourself the following questions several times slowly and in sequence, taking care not to simply repeat your previous answers but to observe again, feel again and describe again:

What is the problem?
- Is there a thought?
- Is there an emotion?
- Is there a body sensation?
- What exactly is it? (Is it a burning sensation, a void, or what? Is it diffuse or sharp?)

When does it occur? (Before the race, at the start, at the gybe mark?)
- Exactly when does it occur?
- Does it occur every time or occasionally? (If occasionally, when?)

Where is the sensation located? (Every thought or emotion has an associated feeling somewhere in the body)
- Exactly where is it located?
- How far beneath the skin is it?

How much is it?
- How large? (A marble, a tennis ball or a football?)
- How strong? Rate it on a 1-10 scale, exactly

Now go back and repeat the whole exercise.

pain in your solar plexus lingers and you become aware of the tightness in your shoulders and the whiteness of your knuckles. How long does it take you to regain your equilibrium, restart your stalled brain and get your body flowing again?

Faced with this situation, I would focus my attention on my hands first, because relaxing the hands tends to trigger relaxation throughout the body. If the feeling was still retained in the solar plexus, I would raise my awareness of that area until it cleared. If thoughts of the recent alarm persisted, I would observe my thoughts until they let go of the 'there and then' and came right back to the 'here and now'.

What? When? Where? How much?

What I have done so far is to advocate raising one's awareness of a problem, and I have illustrated this with an example. The concept can be applied to many situations by employing an exercise which you can both try now and use on board. It is the What? When? Where? How Much? exercise, which requires you to focus an imaginary microscope on the primary manifestation of the problem to be tackled.

To practise, recall in your imagination a recurring problem that arises when you are sailing. Run over a typical incident in your mind's eye as vividly and completely as you can, and proceed with the exercise in the box above as if it was happening here and now.

If this exercise seems too complex to employ in the heat of a race, let me assure you that in time a quick series of What? When? Where? How much? questions can become quite auomatic. Once you have mastered it some key areas or triggers will emerge for you – in my case, for example, I only have to focus on my hands from the inside, and my whole body relaxes.

Some internal obstacles, such as lack of motivation, boredom or obstinacy are not so easy to work on in this way, for it requires highly-developed sensitivity to experience them as anything other than thoughts. However, we can raise our awareness of them, and the What? When? Where? How much? routine can still be applied to thoughts. Some of these problems will be examined in the chapter on Goals.

Note that the exercise does not ask Why? This is because to do so just increases the level of confusing mental activity, leading to analysis which is seldom helpful.

Some internal obstacles may be too persistent and pervasive to be eliminated easily by these methods. They keep recurring, and we begin to notice them in other areas of our life. These problems are related to basic life attitudes established in childhood. As far as each of us is concerned these attitudes simply reflect the way life is, or the way we are. It does not occur to us that they are personal and subjective and can, if necessary, be changed. This is the subject of the next chapter.

4　We are not what we think

Our basic life attitudes influence our learning, our enjoyment and our success – in sailing and in life – more than any other single factor. We all have fundamental attitudes towards life, and therefore to all our activities, and although we may be only vaguely aware of them they are often obvious to our friends. Basic optimism or pessimism, for example, will dramatically affect our lives and the quality of our experience. Indeed, the way we perform any activity is likely to reveal much about the way we manage our lives. You may readily accept that a change in your life attitudes could improve your sailing, but did you realise that an improvement in your approach to, and

therefore success in, your sailing could improve your life?

Try answering the questions in the box below. Your responses will indicate your general outlook on life on the positive/negative, optimist/pessimist scale, but there are a host of more subtle attitudes that we bring to the variety of situations we encounter in sport and in life. Identifying them and acknowledging their existence takes us a long way towards mastering them. We will probably never completely rid ourselves of such attitudes, but we can learn to gain dominion over them and not be a victim to them.

So how can learning more about yourself help you to improve your sailing results?

Basic life attitudes

We all know the one about the wine bottle which is either half full or half empty depending on your attitude. Which view do you take? Here are some other questions to ask yourself, to discover more about your attitudes.

- It is raining hard in the country and you have half an hour to kill. Do you pull on your boots and raincoat and go out and enjoy the freshness, or do you stay at home and complain about the weather?
- Your car has a puncture. Do you decide that all cars are more trouble than they are worth, or that it was just bad luck – and a nail?
- The case of a corrupt policeman fills the news for day. Do you immediately develop a mistrust of all policemen?
- Your three-year-old son trips and falls on the stairs. Do you insist that he holds your hand on the stairs until he is four, or do you encourage him to try again?
- A new club member beats you in her first race after joining. Do you decide that she is always going to beat you, and that you are no good and never will be? Or do you simply accept that she beat you on that occasion, and look forward to the next race?

Suppose you're the type who always views wine bottles as half empty, and you are sailing neck and neck with a rival. Taking your natural pessimistic view you'll probably assume he's pulling away: sure enough the reality soon lives up to your expectation. If this situation recurs a few times you soon get to the point where you will always drop back when someone is alongside, *however slow he is.*

If you recognise that you have the half-empty tendency, you're more likely to be able to see things as they really are. When someone's alongside, you can evaluate relative trends more accurately, and perhaps check your view against your crew's and be willing to accept his opinion.

In short, recognising, continuing to recognise, and choosing to overcome your pessimistic tendency limits its potential to hurt your performance. Remember: the starting point of improvement, success or change is an accurate assessment of where you are.

Although it's difficult to change a life attitude such as timidity, for example, you can adopt another attitude for the duration of a race and see if it works. For a timid person, an appropriate bolt-on attitude would be 'How would I sail in this race if I were a bold competitor?' If this gets results during the race, and you recognise that your timidity is limiting you in other walks of life, you may decide that you really want to change that tendency. But there is truth in the old joke: 'How many psychiatrists does it take to change a light bulb?' Answer: 'Even ten cannot do it unless the light bulb really wants to be changed . . .'

Self image

In addition to certain charactistics, attitudes or tendencies, we each have a self-image which is usually a misconception – but which profoundly affects both our perception and our effectiveness.

The problem with a self-image is that we tend to conform to it. A negative self-image clearly makes bad things worse. Adopting a notion such as 'I am no good at sport' or 'I have no ball sense' creates a self-perpetuating cycle that has to be broken. Unfortunately an overly positive self-image does not help as much as you might expect because arrogance stands in the way of learning. You are unlikely to learn much if you believe you are the best sailor in the world!

As always, realism is the key. An accurate and aware self-perception is the ideal. One way to start is to apply descriptive rather than judgemental terms to yourself. 'I am no good' is not a very helpful observation if you want to improve. On the other hand 'I am enthusiastic, and a precise helmsman, but an erratic tactician and a poor loser' is a useful description, and not only points to problem areas but also indicates strengths upon which to build. In fact any description of your self-image should conclude with 'I am what I am right now, and I have infinite potential'.

This statement really contains the good news, because although we have various characteristics, tendencies, attitudes, self-images, jealousies and all sorts of sometimes unsavoury aspects, deep down we are none of these things. And as we learn that they ebb and flow like the tides, we become aware that beneath it all there is a part of us that is unchanging. It is like a nucleus that remains stable as we display all the parts of ourselves. By cultivating an awareness of the nucleus we can develop the art of detachment from the effects of both our passing emotions and our more persistent attitudes, and so empower ourselves. This nucleus is the source of our very best performances, and nowhere does this show up more than in sport. This is really who we are.

5 The joy of learning

How does a child learn to walk? He sees others doing it and simply plays around with walking until he finds the way that works best for him. It comes naturally, or through what we might call his natural mind. It's an effective method – no-one has walking lessons and everyone learns to walk pretty well. The learning child is not consumed with self-criticism or self-instruction, which become great obstacles to learning as soon as we begin to fear failures. Once this fear takes hold we tend to stop experimenting and as a result learning stops too. 'I wouldn't pull my cunningham on as hard as he does, because I might go slower' is not a very helpful attitude, because you learn something every time you carry out an activity in a different way. What's more, learning what *doesn't* work is just as valuable as learning what *does* work. Maybe you will go slower with a tight cunningham, but at least you've proved it for sure. Maybe you should now try having it slacker than normal? And if that doesn't work either, you'll *know*

Below: Focused awareness is the best tutor.

you were right, and you can stop worrying about that particular control.

Experimenting

Sailing performance is about adapting constantly to changes in the wind and the water. If you have used a variety of settings in practice, on the day of the competition you will be more sensitive to what is needed and you will also be better able to cope if you're inadvertently sailing with the wrong setting. Perhaps I can illustrate this point best with an example from skiing. Most people try hard to have their weight on the correct foot at all times, but bad weather and unexpected terrain will often throw the best of skiers onto the wrong foot. If they have practised skiing on the wrong foot they will be much more confident in awkward conditions. Besides, experimenting is always interesting and interest sustains the awareness upon which learning depends.

Experimentation plus . . .

Experimentation with awareness is the key to learning. So often as soon as we find *one* way of doing something we adopt it as

---

Experimentation

Here are a few exercises you might try, which will help you break out of the mould.

- Try tacking on lifts instead of headers
- Swap crews with another boat
- Try racing in another class
- Swap sails
- Rake the mast aft
- Change roles within the boat
- Swap roles. Give a different person the authority for strategy, or tactics, or tuning.
- Spend the last half-hour before the race in a different way
- Try a different way of deciding where to start
- Alter your final approach to the startline; for example, take a longer or shorter run at it
- Deliberately change your attitude. First, describe yourself as a sailor in one word such as 'cautious'. Next, decide on the opposite: 'bold'. Try sailing the next race as if you were bold. At each stage, imagine what a bold sailor would do next – then do it!
- Try to devise an exercise for your pet weakness. You may worry a lot about manoeuvring before the start in the mêlée of boats. Try looking at the water *between* the boats rather than at all those hulls. (In fact this makes more sense, because we usually go where we're looking). Your nervousness will evaporate, because there *is* room. You can see the possibilities, not the problems, and peripheral vision is not only adequate to deal with possible collisions, it actually gives a quicker response because it keys into the automatic part of your brain. (Direct vision often leads to analysis for which there may be insufficient time, before it inspires action).

the way. We cease looking for other ways, and as we repeat *the* way it becomes more and more familiar so that any other way feels awkward. Even if what we first found was the best way, we have lost flexibility and the experience of alternatives that might be so beneficial in freak conditions or following the failure of some piece of equipment. The chances are, however, that we did not find the best way to do it first time around, due to insufficient awareness. Now we have a habit to break, which makes learning a new way even harder. And so it goes. It need not be that way if we are willing to be patient, aware and humble.

Awareness will tell you the best way far more efficiently than any stopwatch or instructor. The key question to ask yourself while trying out ways of doing something is 'What is happening'. The question you will always be tempted to ask instead is 'What am I doing wrong?' which only increases anxiety. In answering 'What is happening' you will need to call upon all your senses, particularly sight, hearing, touch and, very importantly, the feeling within your own body. Try as far as possible to assimilate this raw pure information and don't pollute it with your critical mind, opinions and analyses. Your natural mind will, without your conscious interference, process far more information far more effectively than you are likely to give it credit for. Trust it – remember that's how you learned to walk.

Experts

What about the knowledge of the experts, all the books by those who are supposed to know and who are so eager to impart their infinite wisdom in equally infinite technical detail? Can I not learn from them, you might ask? Of course you can, a lot, but use it appropriately and beware of the pitfalls. By definition an expert is someone who has experience, but this is usually confined to the activity itself and rarely extends to the art of teaching.

Sailing is a complex sport, and the point about experts can be made clearer by using an example from golf. If on the way out to the tee for your first lesson, the pro were to tell you the seven golden rules of golf, he might well in so doing destroy your golf for ever – even if his rules were totally valid. The reason for this is that he is passing you several covert messages as well:

- That golf is complicated, therefore difficult
- That he knows and you don't, making you feel inferior
- That you are stupid because already you can't remember them all
- That he expects you to be able to employ them all from the start

There are more messages but these will be enough to fill your head with doubts and fears, and to inhibit any natural swing to the ball that you might have had.

How much better it would be if he were to walk out with you, reminding you that you have played with sticks and stones and hit and kicked other balls before, and that this is pretty much the same. He might then drop a few balls on the ground and invite you to just have a go. With no expectations or inhibitions I guarantee you would hit several of them surprisingly well. This would encourage you, make you feel good about yourself and help you to realise that maybe golf is not as hard as 'they say'. Now you are on the way to success.

The pro should at this stage be careful not to praise those first shots too much or he will make you think you were lucky or special, and your anxiety or expectations will rise. He should just take it for granted, get you to hit some more and begin to ask you how it feels, how your body feels, whether the ball is going where you expect it to or towards the point you are aiming at, if you are. Do your feet seem to be in a comfortable position relative to the ball? What about your hands on the club and how free does your swing feel? In answering these questions, or rather in your gathering of the information or feedback to answer them, you are raising your awareness of what is happening. Unbeknown to you, many corrections are already taking place in your body. This is the beginning of the inner approach to learning and the one that I strongly advocate. Of course it demands that the pro keeps his knowledge, his helpful advice and his ego in check, which is too much to expect of many of them.

Expertise

Lest you think I have no time for experts let me show how you can use them. If you had nothing but a dinghy and its rig, no books, no teacher and you had never even seen someone sail, you would learn. However, you would also be reinventing the wheel. You would have no visual images to build upon and you would have no yardstick by which to measure what you had learned. The books and experts do give you valuable guidelines and some parameters, but instead of taking their word as gospel and learning it by rote as if you needed it to pass an exam, use it as a basis to experiment with.

Find out if what they recommend works best for you and under which circumstances. The most physically comfortable way of doing things is almost always the most efficient and effective – and it will coincide in large measure with the textbook. After all, in the beginning people learned how to do new things by experience, and those who did them best wrote the first textbooks. Every human being is constructed slightly differently however, and so one would expect effective styles to vary slightly from person to

person. Remember that your interpretation of the experts' words and the differences between their bodies, their boats, their crews and yours are already going to cause some variation. If you, by experimentation, find out the variations that work best for you under all circumstances and conditions you will be well on course to becoming a skilled, flexible and sensitive sailor. You will now know from your own experience, rather than from their words, why they do what they do and you can become the author of your own book. Bjorn Borg, Jean-Claude Killy and many other outstanding performers in many sports have been successful not because they followed the manual, but because they went beyond it.

It is obvious that the more physically active one's sport is, the more important natural body movements are. Therefore in sailing this will apply more to dinghy sailors than to larger yachtsmen – or rather, to sailors of larger yachts! However, the fundamental principles – flow, ease and economy of movement, concentration and relaxation, focus and commitment – apply to the use of the mind just as they do to the use of the body; hence their relevance to all types of sailing.

How you apply these principles in your sailing is up to you to work out for yourself, for I cannot write your book either. What I am trying to do is to suggest a constructive attitude towards learning that will stand you in good stead throughout your sailing career.

Summary

There is no doubt that learning is faster, more permanent and more precise if it occurs by experience and in a high state of awareness. Learning by rote or in a mechanistic way from books or authoritarian instructors is neither effective nor enjoyable. Both learning and enjoyment are at their best when one is experiencing something to the full in the here and now – and without suffering instruction and criticism from yourself or others. If your thoughts are on what you should do in the future, or on what you did wrong in the past, you are not experiencing the present, and nor are you learning from it or enjoying it.

Criticism and self-criticism

Most of us have at some time or another, especially when we are learning something new, heard a little voice in our heads which says things like 'Do it like this, put your left hand . . . oh no, not like

Below: Let your body do the sailing.

that, stupid. Can't you do anything right?' and adds as an after-thought, 'you might as well give up sailing, you'll never be any good'. Recognise it? So who is talking to whom? Obviously one part of you does not trust another part of you very much. It is also obvious that the part that does *not* do things (your mind) is instructing and criticising the part that *does* do things (your body). That is crazy because your mind has never hit a golf ball, climbed a mountain or steered a boat; it has no experience of doing any of it, but your body certainly has. The body has a large filing cabinet of experiences to draw upon when it wants to do something, but this is only as useful as the quality of information in the files. This is why awareness is so important. The mind is performing a really

useful function when it is inserting accurate information feedback into the files, but if it puts in incorrect or fuzzy information, or merely a vague statement like 'that was wrong or bad', what is going to come out later?

Of course, in indicating that the two parts of ourselves are our minds and our bodies, I am vastly over-simplifying; another and perhaps more representative way of characterising the split is as the anxious mind (the critic) and the natural mind (the doer). It is really helpful to calm the anxious mind as much as we can and stop it chattering, but it won't just shut up.

The solution is to keep it fully occupied filing useful information, or to send it off to amuse itself listening to the sound of the hull on the water, or something equally innocuous. Don't let it do your sailing for you, because it has never done it before and it only knows how to do it *in theory*.

As if our anxious mind is not enough some of us actually pay professional critics to give us even more of that stuff from the outside. If you ever employ an instructor or act as one professionally, or for a friend, do bear this in mind. The hardest lesson any instructor has to learn is when to shut up – which is most of the time.

6 Preparation

If you are serious about racing, you will be doing all you can to get your boat and gear up to scratch for the new season. You may as well get your mind and body in good order while you are about it.

Training – why don't you do it?

Everyone knows that physical training makes you sail faster. Not only does a fit body work better (and longer), but your mental attitude will be enhanced if you know you're fit, and your self-esteem will go up. Yet very few racers train. If you ask them why they don't, you will hear a fascinating range of rationalisations. The truth is that they are too lazy and they are not fully committed. That is not wrong, it is just a fact that has consequences. The answer is to train anyway!

Pick your own medicine: running, swimming, or aerobics. Some people think that sailing is the only training you need for sailing. In fact most forms of sailing do not involve enough exercise to have much training value. You need to be fit to be a good sailor, but sailing will not make you fit unless you go in for one of the most strenuous forms such as boardsailing. Running, swimming and aerobics build up your stamina; they will also improve your flexibility and, incidentally, greatly reduce the chances of developing heart disease.

Tiredness

Let us assume that you do train and you are in relatively good shape physically, but you still get tired. What is happening? Tiredness comes as much from the body's internal struggle against its own tension as it does from the excercise itself. It stands to reason that, if 20 per cent of your energy is unconsciously devoted to tensing up your body, only 80 per cent of your energy is available for action. However a further 20 per cent of the total is required to overcome the existing tension, which now begins to look like sabotage. The result of this is that only 60 per cent of your energy is available for the job. To compensate for this loss you try harder, which in turn increases the tension you have to overcome. So the exhausting vicious circle continues. Learn to relax and your stamina will increase a hundredfold. Remember that the tension stems from thoughts and feelings and that is the level at which it has to be tackled – with awareness.

The rules

Not knowing the rules shows a lack of commitment and an avoidance of responsibility but don't get obsessive about them – and don't ever become a dinghy-park lawyer. Just get a good book on the subject (such as *The Rules in Practice* by Bryan Willis) and study it.

Tuning before . . .

Perhaps the hardest thing about tuning your boat is knowing when to stop and get on with sailing it. By all means experiment: try moving your mast and your rudder forward and back, try sailing the windward leg with the centreboard raised different amounts, try varying the tension on your jib halyard and practise alongside a mate with a flat sail with your sail full, and vice versa. Do all these things so you know their effects by experience, and not just by repute. Your adjustments in the race will then be just a matter of fine tuning – with confidence.

While you are experimenting with the tuning of your boat, you will find that the greater your awareness of your own senses, the finer you will be able to tune. As you become a more experienced sailor, and a better one, you will demand a more finely-tuned boat. Awareness will shorten the time you take to become experienced, and

Below: Tune your rig – and your perceptions.

it will also give you a more efficient boat to do it in.

But now stop tuning, perhaps as much as two weeks before a big race, and go out and sail the boat.

Familiarisation

It may be a luxury, but if you get to a regatta a day early you will be much more relaxed. It is not that you specifically need to learn your way around, but familiarity with one's environment, even the restaurants, the moorings, the dinghy park and the toilets, frees the mind to focus on the other essential preparatory tasks. Coping with new surroundings is work for the mind, even if it is stimulating in a way. The sooner you can slot some of it away into automatic the better.

If it is a big regatta, you might try running over the pre-race scene in your mind's eye in as much detail as you can, several times before you get there. It will help with familiarisation if you have been there before, even if it was only in your mind. It certainly works for animals. Horses being entered for Olympic dressage events have been played tape recordings of the roar of a crowd, traffic noise and loudspeaker commentaries for a week or so prior to such competitions and the familiarising effect has been found to be invaluable. Playing your own mental tapes may be good for you too.

Mental rehearsal

Mental practice is an invaluable learning tool you can usefully borrow from the experts. Many athletes lie in bed the night before an event running the course in their mind's eye. The great skier Jean-Claude Killy always did this. He told me that on one occasion he saw himself fall at a particular gate. He re-ran his mental movie again and again until he negotiated

Mental rehearsal

The way I would rehearse mentally for a sailing race would go something like this. I would sit in a chair with my eyes closed for quarter of an hour imagining myself going around the course. Say I'm coming up to the gybe mark. I observe myself and the boat in as much detail as possible. I complete the gybe. Now I re-run it again several times, letting the image become clearer. Note I'm *not* trying to make the gybe better each time – I'm just observing it closely. If any part of the movement is fuzzy, that's a sure sign I'm indecisive at that point, so I concentrate on that next time. Eventually the whole gybe is focused, smooth and successful. I run it through a couple more times to channel it into my mind, then go on with the next leg. At the end I would mentally run the whole course several times to integrate the parts.

the gate perfectly. In the race next day his performance was flawless.

Thinking about the race the night before is not neurosis, it has a useful function. In visualising you are *practising*. Research has shown that mental rehearsal is the next best thing to physical practice and easy and cheap to do anywhere! In one experiment which took place over three weeks basketball players of similar standard were divided into three groups. Group 1 spent some time practising shooting baskets. Group 2 spent the same time visualising themselves shooting successfully. Group 3 was a control group that did neither. At the end of the experiment there was little to choose between the performances of Groups 1 and 2, but both were now some 20 per cent better than Group 3.

Mental preparation

Don't carry mental garbage into the race. Do whatever you need to do ahead of time to have a clear mind when the race starts. This might entail writing your will before you set off on the Fastnet, wiggling the pintles to see if the rudder is going to stay put, or climbing the mast to check for cracks. It's obviously distracting to have had a row with someone just before you go

afloat. If you did, clear it up – phone to say you're sorry or send flowers. If you have a problem that can't be solved, set it on one side before you start. If you do not fully succeed, all is not lost, for if you really focus your attention on the job in hand the problem should be swept away, at least temporarily.

Checking

One way to limit anxiety is to use a responsible system of checks to go over your gear thoroughly before each race. Then let go of it. People have a neurotic tendency to return to their checking; 'I wonder if. . .' will quickly take your attention away from where it should be.

Routines

I know of one very meticulous sailor whose idea of race preparation is to get out on the course early and sail the first beat twice, checking windshifts, currents and his rig settings. Then, happy that he's done all he can, he's ready for the hassle of the startline.

Imagine his feelings when he was invited to helm a boat with a completely different ethos. The new crew's routine was to stay ashore till the last possible moment, motor to the startline in a rush and put the sails up just before the gun. Whatever he did, he couldn't persuade them to be out there early, or do any pre-start work. The mis-match of attitudes meant everyone had a miserable regatta.

No routine is right or wrong. The only question to ask is, does it serve you well? Presumably the crew had, some time in the past, arrived late at the start (and thus with no expectations), by a fluke hit the line at the right spot, had a good race and finished well. This was then adopted as a routine.

One approach to this problem would be to delve into the real reason behind their routine, and then ask how well it served them. On the plus side, they're familiar with it, so it helps them keep calm. On the negative side, they don't have an opportunity to check the wind on the course. And in this particular instance the helmsman could not (in his opinion) operate to his full potential.

A good solution might have been for the helmsman to suggest they give his approach to try. If things didn't improve after a few races, they could always go back to their old technique. But my guess is they would enjoy trying something new. You can learn a lot if you're prepared to sacrifice your sacred cows.

The start

It is not for me, nor is it the intention of this book, to tell you precisely how to make a good start, but I can offer pointers and indicate areas to watch which may affect your mental state, and therefore your ability to start well consistently.

Each individual racer quickly settles into a habitual starting routine, probably repeating many elements of what he or she happened to do in their very first race if it went reasonably well, or the exact opposite if it didn't. Familiarity is helpful for relaxation, but it is easy to make a habit out of doing the wrong thing.

Go on experimenting with your starts so that when and if you settle for a particular way, you have at least tried all the options. Certainly some elements need to become routine, like your pre-race checks. Be careful though, for habit dulls awareness. Can you combine the relaxing qualities of a familiar situation with the perception that accompanies a new experience?

Remember that if you are not over the line early every now and then, you are probably not trying hard enough.

Below: Check the boat thoroughly before the race – then stop worrying about it.

Certainly you will not be practising how to hit it right on the button. Be prepared to lose a few; take a risk or two in races that do not matter too much. Some people always start further back because they feel obliged to submit to some imaginary fleet pecking order, but then again such a person would not have bought this book.

If you do manage to get a great start and find yourself at the head of the fleet, don't get carried away; there is a long way to go. Settle down to alert fast sailing right away. The start is already history; come back to the here and now.

Tuning during . . .

Now here you are in the race and you decide objectively that you really are going slowly. You're confronted by hundreds of choices. Should you sail high and slowly or low and fast? How's the rig? What about the centreboard? Your anxious mind is in a fit of indecisiveness, and in a hurry to sort out the problem. So what should you do?

Half the problem is a lack of willingness to give yourself time to decide what to do. When you have decided (and it doesn't really matter what you choose) make an immediate alteration. Then *give it time to take effect*. If it's wrong, you can always go back to the old setting. Don't forget to alter all the other things that go hand in glove with your chosen change (if you harden the mainsheet you may need to drop the traveller to keep the boom on the centreline). At this stage anxiety about whether you've made the right decision can of itself cause you to go slower, so either concentrate on one of the speed exercises described in the next chapter, or think about something divorced from sailing. When you have calmed down, observe what's happening then act again if necessary.

How big an alteration should you make? For example, if you're on maximum rig tension, how much should you let off? The answer is, within reason, plenty; that way you're sure to get an alteration of speed. You might drop two-thirds of the way down your calibrated range, and see what happens.

Meanwhile watch out you don't become obsessed with rig tension; this is only an experiment, after all.

Tuning often seems to be all thought and worry. Can it ever be automatic? By now you probably know that the answer is a resounding 'yes'. If you are used to tuning the boat, and have plenty of tuning skills in your mental filing cabinet, your natural mind will tune the boat beautifully. Just as with boatspeed, when you're on automatic your mind is perfectly focused and at its most efficient. This is what the old pro is doing when he just sets the sail up till it 'looks right'. But measure it if you can and you'll find it is right too.

7 Optimum performance

As part of my research for this book I spent a day racing in a hot one-design fleet in the Solent. From my perch on the weather rail I was able to watch the helmsman (Tim Davison) closely, and see a perfect example of mental processess in action.

The line was square, we started well (in the middle) and the whole fleet blasted off on a long starboard tack. No one was close enough to interfere with us, and whether or not we drew ahead of the pack was clearly going to be up to Tim: as he put it 'It's up to the mut on the end of the tiller'.

For a while things went well. Tim's posture was relaxed, he held the tiller lightly and his eyes moved steadily from jib luff to compass. We gradually pulled ahead of the neighbouring boats. Then he looked under the boom, and the rot set in.

'Those guys to the leeward are really motoring. Do you reckon there's less tide down there? Or are we going like a brick?' He raised the traveller an inch or two, tightened his grip on the tiller and started to tweak the mainsail controls. A glance over his weather shoulder did nothing to improve morale – the boats up there were beginning to sail over us.

'Get some more weight forward and let off the jib halyard a bit, can you', he said between clenched teeth, wiggling the tiller erratically to try and push the boat through the waves. He was hunched forward, his face muscles rigid and his eyes tense. He clearly wasn't enjoying this!

Another glance over his shoulder. 'Do you reckon the right side of the course could be quicker? We're going to have to go anyway, we're being lee-bowed. Ready?

Let's go.' We tacked, ducking transoms and heading out to the wrong side of the course in a search for clear air, in the vague hope that we might be going the right way. We weren't. By the time we tacked back the leaders were way out to the left, well ahead and our race was over almost before it had begun.

When Tim started he was relaxed and confident. His natural mind was sailing the boat and we were going well. A moment of self-doubt allowed his anxious mind to take over. Not only did it destroy his boatspeed, but it panicked him into quick decisions about tactics, tuning and strategy.

Phasing

Tim in that instant fell prey to most of the problems we have already discussed, but he was also panicked into moving too quickly from one aspect of sailing to another. In fact no-one's mind is good at doing more than one thing at a time. The ideal is to *phase*, that is spend 30 seconds focused on one simple task, 30 seconds on the next, and so on.

When you're racing, your mind will phase by dwelling for a while on helming, then tuning, then strategy, and finally tactics before returning to helming. Note that the time in each phase is not the same: Ed Baird reports that upwind he spends only 15 per cent of his time in boatspeed phase, and the rest on his position relative to other boats. Downwind he spends 85 per cent of his time on speed.

In this chapter I want to look at how your mind behaves when it's in the speed phase.

Heel

The angle of the forestay to the horizontal is a vital speed indicator for many yacht helmsmen. Block the line of sight forward, and speed drops dramatically.

Sail hard on the wind on one tack for several minutes. Every few seconds rate your heel on a scale of 0-10: 0 for upright and 10 for the masthead hitting the water. Say the scores out loud if it helps . . . 'Two, two, one, three . . . ' Don't try and aim for a score or keep the scores constant, just concentrate on recording as accurately as possible what the heel is. You are heightening your consciousness, maximising the filing away of experience, letting your body be absorbed in the way the boat feels at various angles of heel, and probably having more fun on a long beat than you thought possible. You may also find you're sailing fast; don't force this, trust your natural mind's ability to process the accurate information it is receiving and move you automatically towards your goal of greater speed to windward.

Note that your anxious mind would probably prefer an inclinometer but what matters is experiencing the heel in your body, not a number on an arbitrary scale, and sailing by feel is certainly more enjoyable. On one occasion Tony Morgan, an Olympic medallist in Flying Dutchmen who had since taken to competing in a Class 1 ocean racer, was my guest at a house I had in the Bahamas. The only sailing boat I had was a 400-dollar Sunfish, but he spent the heat of the day beating up and down the bay in a strong wind. When he returned, exhausted, I asked him whether he could have had that much fun in his yacht and he replied 'Never, in this I can feel every ripple and every gust right through my body'. The bonus is that as you develop the feel you become far better equipped to compensate for changes and cope with emergency.

Telltales

Beat for a while watching the telltales near the jib luff. Don't *try* to keep them streaming, just observe them continuously and let the helm correct itself (As your awareness increases, this will happen automatically.)

Automatic sailing

Since three-quarters of your time is going to be spent concentrating on the non-helming phases, it's vital to develop automatic helming skills. Then when you're trying to fathom which side of the course to head for your boatspeed won't drop too much. (In fact, as we'll see later, it may even increase!)

Learning to sail fast automatically is a bit like learning to walk automatically. You simply do lots and lots of practice, gradually building up a huge mental filing cabinet of experiences which can be drawn on later when your conscious mind is occupied elsewhere.

The problem for most people is that although they practice walking every day of their lives, they only work on their sailing for a few weekends each year. To bump up the amount of experience filed away during a limited practice session, the

The tiller

Still on a beat, concentrate on the feel of your hand where it meets the tiller. Rate on some self-devised scale how hard you're pulling the helm and stay with it for as long as it interests you.

Listening

Listen to the sound of the bow cutting through the water. Really listen, as you would to a piece of music that you like. You ride with it rather than just check on it every now and again. Can you hear the bow hit each wave crest? Listen to the silence between. What does it sould like in a trough? Is there a difference as you luff and bear away? Can you hear the boat speed up or slow down? What happens to the sound as she heels?

Visualising

Can you visualise the bow cutting through the water cleanly and efficiently? Shut your eyes, if it helps. Hold this visual image for as long as you can.

The compass

Now watch the compass as you beat. Sing out the readings over a period: '120, 125, 130, 125, 130 . . . ' Then try it on a run, keeping the boat at the best angle to the wind.

Waves

On a beat, reach or run say 'trough, crest, trough, crest . . . ' at the *exact* moment that the bow reaches them.

Mainsheet traveller

When beating, keep your hand lightly on the tiller and steer with the traveller. Note the position of the slider relative to the centre point, and say 'up 10cm, down 5, up 20 . . . '

secret is to heighten your awareness while you're in action.

Speed exercises

In tennis, the ball is the focal point of the game. In skiing, the inside edge of your downhill ski is where the real action takes place. To improve in these sports you must heighten your awareness of the ball or the feel of that edge. But what is the focus of the game in sailing? The answer is that it could be in one of a number of places depending on whichever works for you. The exercises above may help.

Here are some of the effects of these exercise that you might notice. Even though I am telling you about them in this example, do not look for these effects. Notice what happens when *you* try the exercises. Expectation will inhibit your capacity to experience freely.

In most activities in life we depend more on our sight than on our other senses. Closing your eyes will increase the sensitivity of your hearing and touch. If, for example, when beating to windward you focus on the sounds alone, your hull speed will tend to increase but you will probably come off the wind. Conversely if you just block your hearing, you will depend even more on sight than usual, with the effect that you end up sailing so close to the wind that you lose boatspeed. Experimenting with this will show you how you gather information and which sense to use for a particular effect.

The sense that we neglect most is feel. As it is neglected, its potential is the least developed, which makes it our most valuable sense for improvement. Close your eyes and block your hearing at the same time, and you will be obliged to depend on the feel of the tiller. You may be surprised how well you can sail. You are likely to maximise the combined efficiency of speed and direction. Your over-compensating tiller movements will reduce by half. Now you will know how to balance out the use of all your senses to the best overall effect.

The focused attention evoked by these exercises is every bit as important as the specifics of the particular exercise. Each exercise occupies your anxious mind usefully, as an information gatherer, allowing your natural mind the freedom to get on with sailing the boat. As I pointed out earlier, that is the way you learned to walk. And look how well you do that.

Anxiety distorts perception

Let's return to the example at the beginning of this chapter. When you're racing in line abreast your anxiety can easily distort the information that you receive. It's hard to tell if the others are really pulling ahead, or if you're imagining it. What you need is pure information, without the emotional charge. Otherwise your fantasy may lead you to play around with the rig and go slower and produce the very thing you fear. The perfect start to an awful vicious circle.

The solution is to increase your concentration on the information coming aboard. If you flood yourself with information, there's no room for anxiety. If you don't know what to do, you haven't enough information. If you have enough information, you'll always know what to do.

Information is just what it says: pure information, without judgement, criticism, analysis, opinions or concern. Lack of information causes anxiety which leads to obsession. You become convinced it's the jib halyard tension that's wrong, despite all evidence to the contrary and to the exclusion of all other variables. Many an aeroplane pilot's obsession with one instrument has caused him to ignore the others with fatal results.

Information from the crew may carry an accusatory overtone. To counteract this, ask them questions that oblige them to focus on information gathering, rather than sliding you veiled backhanders. 'OK, if they're going faster you can see why? How are they sheeting their jib? What sails have they got up? How much are they heeling?'

Anxiety often rises to fever pitch when people start catching up from astern. Sometimes there's nothing you can do about it, particularly if the wind is filling in from behind. The secret is simply to accept it, and say to yourself that you're going to go as fast as you can given the wind you're in. You can't do any better than the best you can do.

Things do tend to go wrong when you find yourself in the lead. Time and again a crew creams round the first lap, only to be buried on the second. This could be because they're getting lazy up front, though it's more likely to be the increasing tension from their impending win. They're probably fantasising about the trophy or the praise they see coming their way. What they have lost is their attention on the present; the prize-giving ceremony is not here yet. The only place you can actually be, and do anything useful, is *here, now*. So be here now.

Concentration on the job . . .

Amazing things happen when you operate at 100 per cent concentration. I used to be a professional racing driver. After a poor

Below: Don't panic when they start catching up from behind . . .

start at Le Mans in 1966, I had to catch up fast early in the race. I came up behind three cars abreast on the Mulsanne Straight and there was no room to overtake them on the road. I was unwilling to wait even for a moment for them to sort themselves out, as it would have cost me my speed all the way down the straight. I eased onto the grass verge and swept by at over 200 mph. I knew I could do it safely. There was never even a question in my mind. 100 per cent concentration and commitment blend into an unstoppable team that can master situations that would certainly be foolhardy for any competitor not experiencing that rare frame of mind.

Tony Morgan recounts in his own words another experience, this time in the

Fastnet, which further illustrates the supranormal capacity that can be attained when opportunity, necessity and commitment converge:

'We had been running under spinnaker in strong to gale force winds from the Fastnet Rock. I had been far too long on the helm, but had actually developed 'with the wind' so to speak, in that each increase in wind strength had been absorbed into my subconscious and all my senses were attuned to the wind and waves. I think my judgement of approaching squalls came from temperature changes on the back of my hair and ears, the sudden changes of tone in the rigging, and the noise of the waves. My automatic responses to these perceptions had undoubtedly kept the boat under the chute and therefore the chute in one piece.

'The professional skipper of *More Opposition* had by now become concerned that I'd been helming for well over time – some two and a half to three hours under heavy conditions – and was anxious to relieve me. His experience was light-years ahead of my own and he was clearly my superior on the boat, and normally I would defer to his judgement, without hesitation. Yet I knew I was experiencing skills outside and beyond my normal ability that had developed with the conditions. I realised that the moment I broke the harmony, a thousand pounds worth of spinnaker would be lost.

'Eventually the professional's argument overcame my intuition, and I succumbed. Within seconds we broached – the spinnaker in ribbons. Years and years of experience were no substitute for the temporary mastery born out of total concentration'.

100 per cent concentration is not tensing up and studying the jib luff with a furrowed brow or trying hard to do something right. It is quite the reverse. It is a state of absolute knowing and absolute trust. It is a very calm state somewhat akin to peak experiences described by mystics and meditators. But it is rare indeed.

... And off it

A more common but no less interesting experience is one that, in many ways, suggests the complete opposite. Have you ever driven along a familiar route completely absorbed in a business problem? Suddenly you are home. Where did those last ten miles go? This is really driving on automatic. In fact your natural mind was fully engaged with driving and probably was at its most efficient. You drove better than usual, not worse as you might think, while your anxious mind was equally fully occupied with cash flows or profit forecasts. This is not to advocate inattentive driving; the state of concentrated attention is vital to good performance but the actual object of that attention does not have to be the job in hand. However, what you concentrate upon will determine what you recall, and in the example of driving in automatic you recall nothing of the route home.

You can sail like this too, if only you can stop your anxious mind from offering unhelpful advice. Give it something useful to do like one of the exercises mentioned earlier, or let it focus upon something completely divorced from sailing just to park it out of the way. Of course, trying hard to get into automatic will never work. Doing one of the concentration/awareness exercises may produce that result but, even if it does not, the focused attention will calm the mind and enhance your performance anyway. All you can do is to create the right conditions. The value lies in the process as much as the result.

It is much harder to go into automatic when the pressure is on. In sailing the ideal might be to make controlling the boat fully automatic while the mind is occupied with race tactics. Conversely focusing fully on race management may allow the sailing of the boat to become fully automatic. Remember that when you are sailing in automatic, that's as efficient as you will ever be, though it takes some practice to learn to trust it. As a learner driver you certainly did not go into automatic. It is the things that you practise most that go into automatic first. They don't say that practice makes perfect for nothing. When golfer Gary Player holed in one some time ago, a spectator commented to him on his luck. 'Yes', he said, 'the more I practise, the luckier I get'.

Tactics

In the same way if you can put your tactics phase into automatic you'll be more efficient and more responsive to a changing situation. Do you really think you can anticipate what moves you'll need to make when you're jockeying with four other boats for the inside turn at a mark? Your anxious mind would be full of the fear of a collision.

We asked several world-class sailors what was going through their minds in a race as they approached the gybe mark in really hairy conditions. Most reported that they were thinking ahead to the next leg, usually the position they wanted ten or twenty lengths past the mark, their actual sailing being left to their natural minds in automatic. None dwelt on the hazards of colliding or capsizing – they obviously trusted their natural minds to take care of that.

And that's the goal to aim for. Yet we lesser mortals do tense up as we close with the buoy and a huge gust hits us just before we make our approach to gybe.

If you're lucky enough to be gybing right behind an expert, it is easy: simply model yourself on his movements. (Note 'model' rather than 'copy' because fluidity is important and if you analyse his movements, break his gybe down into parts, you're going to be jerky). If there isn't an expert handy, simply imagine yourself doing a perfect gybe – and do it!

Then give your natural mind an image of where you want to be ten lengths after the mark (ahead, and to windward), and let it work out all the permutations and combinations. Longer-term tactics and overall race strategy are obviously of a more prescribed mental nature, but that does not mean that awareness does not apply. Self-awareness may be critical: for example, you should be aware of your own resistance to abandoning or altering a strategy when it becomes appropriate to do so.

Relaxation on board

When you're on automatic you're relaxed in body, and in mind too if it is in a passive receptive mode – as it would be if you were listening to the bow cutting the water. Working on race tactics would certainly be more mentally taxing, but if you have removed much of the other workload, even that could be quite relaxing.

This state of relaxed concentration, which at first sounds like a contradiction in terms, is what we seek to cultivate. In this state performances, learning and enjoyment are each at their optimum. If either your performance or your enjoyment is off, and this applies to any activity, not just sailing, check which of the following familiar essential ingredients is missing. Invariably one or more will be, and you will know what to work on.

Awareness This is a passive receptive, rather than a doing, state. It is a condition of feelings rather than of thoughts. It is pure experience, without judgement, criticism, opinions or analysis. (Obviously this is not totally true if you are developing tactics or working on navigation, though the principle still holds.)

100 per cent commitment This may require adjusting your short term goals and is closely allied to, but not identical to, concentration. It is probably the single most important factor in competition.

Trust Not trying hard. Trust of yourself, your natural mind and your inate ability.

8 Myths and realities

The job of a sportsman is to produce his own best performance and it's a manifestation of inadequacy or self-doubt to resort to psychologically undermining your competitors. However, a few people will inevitably do this, so you need some ways of resisting them. But first of all, be sure that they are doing it. Who really psychs who?

Being psyched out – or not

Eric Twiname was a marvellous sailor. In the 1970s he had enormous success in the Laser class, including winning a National Championship. But I must say that his boat *Serendipity* was the scruffiest in the fleet. She was unceremoniously dumped on the beach at the end of each day's racing, the bottom was only slightly less pitted than the lunar surface, and the sail was screwed up in the cockpit. I don't think it had ever been folded in its life.

The effect on Eric's rivals was amazing. They wondered how he could possibly win in an old crate like that, and worried about how fast he'd go if he ever bought a new boat. I don't know if anyone took to roughening his own hull or jumping up and down on his sail, but that sort of thing was in the air. Eric just smiled, and kept on winning.

Note how Eric's *habit* was picked up by the other sailors and made into their own fantasy. Who knows why Twiname preferred sailing an old boat? Maybe he couldn't afford a new one: maybe he reckoned all Lasers go at the same speed anyway; maybe he had a sentimental

attachment to that old boat or maybe he was just lazy when it came to maintenance. Whatever it was, he had a system which worked for him. He probably would have gone faster in a new boat, if he could have got round his superstition or whatever it was. That was *his* problem. But, by allowing the whole idea to have a psyching effect on them, the other racers made it *their* problem. It became something he did to them. Eric's habit became their fantasy.

Even if someone is deliberately trying to psych you, the way to overcome it is just the same as for so many problems I have discussed; focus 100 per cent on the job to be done. After all, as I already asked, who psychs who? Any psyching is done by yourself to yourself. It's impossible to psych someone who is unwilling to co-operate or is too occupied to allow it to affect him.

Other people in the boat may be susceptible to psyching too, particularly during inactive periods. In one race we were starting on a line which must have been nearly a mile long. We were so absorbed with our pre-start routine that it wasn't until three or four minutes before the start that we realised the bulk of the fleet was down at the other end of the line. Immediately the crew's anxiety boiled over. What are we doing here? Why are they down there? We're going to be last!

If you allow an argument to develop at this stage about the merits of each end of the line you're certain to make a poor start at your end. The reality of the situation is that you haven't time to sail to the other end anyway; you have presumably thought hard about where to start so you must now back your judgement. The answer is for the skipper to take hold of the crew's attention and focus it on something that matters, such as watching transits or setting up the boat for the start. It's a waste of time concentrating on something you can't do anything about.

Why is he starting there? Why do they have a number 2 genoa up? Why are they gybing now? Why indeed – maybe even they don't know quite why they are doing it. Arguments and counter-arguments going on among the crew or within one's own head are a source of anxiety, which is why I try to avoid the 'why?' questions. Any solution you give to the question 'why?' is unlikely to be more than a fantasy. Sometimes you may get it right and sometimes it may help, but generally not. In any case they divert your attention from the job in hand. Simply treat such actions as information and don't get paranoid about why they are doing it. You will never really know and it does not matter anyway.

The whole point of examining the internal factors that this book is largely about is to get rid of the obstacles which are blocking your own best performance. If you are busy being psyched out by other people – or doing the same to them – you can't be focused 100 per cent on the job in hand. Come back to the normal concentration drills (see chapter 7) and put your attention where it can do most good.

Note that *none* of the top performers is where he is because of psyching although anyone may occasionally resort to it in a moment of weakness. John McEnroe became one of the world's greatest sports stars through being a wonderful tennis player, not because of his tantrums.

If your fleet is heavily into playing games, just get on with the race in your own way. Some of the others may change to follow your example, and the racing will become a lot more enjoyable.

Pecking order

Time and again you hear of sailors changing class and winning their first race. Often they do well in the second one, too. But gradually they learn who are the hot racers in that fleet, and their results deteriorate. As they come up through the field they get behind someone who always beats them, or they feel ought to beat them. Then they just sit there. And it's almost as destructive to come up behind someone they know is a rabbit. They're expecting to get by, and quickly, so disappointment and anxiety increase if they don't zoom past.

The game we should play is all about here and now. But the pecking order is about there and then. What happened in the last six races is irrelevant to this one. Simply look at each race in isolation, and the self-perpetuating order will disappear. Treat each boat as a challenge, ignoring her sail number and crew, and just ask how you're going to get by it. Even the world champion may have a hangover or partial gear failure – you just can't tell what's happening on any boat.

The game of being Number One

'He walked into the bar like a young champion. Slow rolling gait, face impassive, perfectly together. Then he stood, still, legs apart, at peace after winning for the third day running'.

How easy it is to assume 'That's the way to do it – I'd better adopt an aloof attitude too if I want to win'. The fact of the matter is that it works for him, and who knows why he's aloof? Maybe his father ignored him when he was three years old. Next year's champion may be the opposite: an extrovert who explains how he does it to anyone who will listen. So are you going to try and be an extrovert now? Obviously you can't blow with the wind – having read this far you hardly need to be told that the previous winner's personality is of no

Above: Forget the personalities in the other boats – just race!

consequence whatsoever to your own task of racing to the best of your own ability.

In the build-up to an early Olympic series it was blowing old boots. Even the assembled experts stayed ashore, not wanting to risk their gear or their egos. Not so the great Dane, Paul Elvstrom. The story has it that he took his customary practice sail and brought the boat back into the harbour on a dead run, exchanging matey banter with the assembled sailors on shore. Then, despite the howling wind and spray he stood up and gybed several times, still carrying on the conversation. Needless to say, at the end of the regatta he collected yet another gold medal.

But why is it needless to say? I'm willing to bet Elvstrom didn't do those gybes to pysch the faint-hearts ashore. If you're really good at something it becomes terribly easy; I'm sure it just seemed like a good thing to do at the time. Beware of reading too much into the actions of the guy at the top.

Hyping yourself

John McEnroe has developed a highly personal technique of arguing with officials when he needs more adrenalin. But although he is one of the best tennis players ever, I have no doubt that he could be better still if he were to find a less destructive way of hyping himself. Most competitors suffer from the opposite problem – too much adrenalin. Whichever is the case for you, the solution is the same as for most internal problems – simply be aware of the level of tension you have. Don't fight it; observe it closely, rate it if you like on a 1 to 5 scale, and it will readjust to the required level quite quickly. Of course if you need to calm down it may help you to walk away from contact with other people and take a peaceful look at the cows grazing in the field behind the dinghy park. In practice most people quite naturally and unconsciously develop their own little rituals which help them to keep in balance. Finding your own is just a matter of doing whatever you feel like doing, however irrational it may seem, and provided that it harms no one else.

Anger

In a light-weather race a power boat churns through the middle of the fleet, kicking up a huge wash and shaking the wind out of a hundred sails. Some crews become quite abusive. Others smile at their purple prose, heel their boats to get the sails back into shape as soon as possible, and press on with the race. Which do you think will pull ahead?

The power boat driver is history. He may be ignorant, bad mannered or a show-off – it doesn't matter. Don't give him your power or let him upset you. The residual conditions are what you're in. They're not good or bad. The only point is, what adjustments do you need to make to *capitalise* on these conditions? As usual, work out exactly where you are (in choppy water) and your goal (good speed in light and lumpy conditions). This calm assessment will occur automatically if you don't let your anxious mind become clogged with anger.

Sulking is the residue of anger. If you're sailing along at the back, hating every minute and mentally writing the 'For Sale' advertisement for your boat, change your goal. Let's try to be 15th. Let's sail as effectively as we can with only half the centreboard. Let's try an extreme outhaul setting. You will at least expand your mastery of the sport by enlarging the range of conditions you feel comfortable in and you will change misery into enjoyment. But you have to be willing to give up indulging yourself in righteous indignation. If you won't do that, go home! There's no disgrace in quitting. Just say 'I quit', at least you'll respect yourself for your honesty.

Intimidation

Starting by the pin, rounding next to a buoy, short-tacking along the shore: often two helmsmen want to be on the same piece of water at the same time. Obviously each wants to do his best, but there comes a point where that commitment can be taken 'to the death'. Your commitment is to winning, not to sinking the boat. In some circumstances it may be necessary to yield.

You may think this is chickening out. But why attach meaning to it? *That* will cause you a problem, and may slow you down for a long time. Sometimes you're going to get the pole position, sometimes not. That's the way it is.

The bogey man

Is there anyone in your fleet who you hate? Who tacks on you every time he crosses you? Who always luffs you on the reach? Who goes out of his way to blanket you on the run? Does he hate you?

Check out yourself first before you start making accusations. Is this reality or a fantasy? The basic rule when you have problems with other people is to start by looking at yourself. Often it will be your fault; maybe not totally but at least partially. You have a problem which you are projecting onto the other guy. After all it is easier to blame someone else than it is to look at our own faults.

If you decide someone is really out to get you, act and act early. Most people express their dissatisfaction by grumbling to their friends, and never speak to the person who really should be hearing the complaint. It's like moaning about the soup to your fellow dinners but telling the restauranteur the meal was just fine. You also want to strike while the iron is hot. If you wait for several races, when you do finally have your showdown you will be very, very aggressive. No, bring it up early, in a civilised way, not necessarily assuming it's his fault.

Take responsibility for the problem. 'I felt that you were tacking on me. Was that so or am I wrong?' How he responds will tell you if he's doing it intentionally or not. With a bit of luck you can discuss it rationally; after all covering at the front of the fleet on the last beat is fair game, whereas sitting on someone in 50th place on the first leg is crazy.

A good example of someone taking positive action on a problem is provided by the Kingston Olympics. Rodney Pattisson (who eventually won the Flying Dutchman Silver Medal) was concerned about a boat constantly covering him. Even if he did a dummy tack the other boat stuck to him like glue. There's nothing against this in the rules, though 'team racing' is against their spirit. Eventually Pattisson wrote to the Olympic Committee who agreed to view the next race. As a result of what they saw they had a word with the team manager of the offending boat, and the problem disappeared.

People are different. Just because you're in a sailing race, you can't expect everyone to conform to the same nuances of racing ethics as you. You might discuss this with your antagonist: 'That's interesting. We differ in what we think sailing is about. . .'

In the very unlikely event that he is acting unreasonably, you may have to accept that his personality and yours are incompatible. But why become a victim? This kind of episode doesn't make you a lesser or a bigger person. Just let the differences run off you. Every so often you will have a problem with this guy – that's just the way it is. If you can't handle that, you can always join another class.

There are a few people who will go to any lengths to win. In one European championship the title hung in the balance between two people – let's call them Tyrant and Victim. In the last race Tyrant organised half a dozen of his countrymen to take out Victim. When everyone else was halfway up the first beat Victim was still on the startline, head to wind, encircled by the stooges. I can report that Tyrant later

collected his trophy in total silence. And never raced in the class again.

Who is in charge of your tactics?

Are you the conductor of your orchestra, or do you react to what others do?

In one big race we were lining up to start right by the inner distance mark. Things were going well – we flapped, inched forward, luffed to prevent anyone barging in between us and the buoy. With 30 seconds to go we were ready to pull in the sheets and go for the line. Imagine our horror when, looking up, we found a huge motor boat, stationary, just over the line, and completely blocking our path. As we reached around her, our start ruined and the crew overcome by rage, the owner of the motor boat nonchalantly leant over the rail and drawled 'Why don't you look where you're going?' Modesty forbids me to tell you our reply.

And yet the man in the blazer and cravat had a point. How could we have missed that huge boat? Once we spotted it, all we could do was react. If we'd been awake and noticed it earlier, we'd have had half a dozen alternatives.

Most successful racers are action people, not reaction people. The extent to which you rely on reaction is the extent to which you are likely to fail.

There is a great difference between reacting and *responding*. On the racecourse you are forever responding to the elements and to the competition. The difference is that in responding you have a choice: by being aware of what's going on around you you give yourself time to choose the best alternative.

The reactors of the fleet end up blaming other people for their mistakes. By blaming that motor boat for our bad start we learned nothing: blame is a good way of staying stuck. But if you can accept responsibility, you can learn: next time we won't concentrate on our start to the exclusion of the rest of the world.

Superstitions

Superstitions are a great trap. If you won your first race in a special T-shirt, and have worn it in every race since, you'll be lost the day it goes missing. It's fine to have your little fads provided you don't attach any importance to them. Being run by a T-shirt is no way to enter a sailing race.

That's a pretty obvious superstition. Others can be more insidious, such as a rigid pre-start routine, having a certain crewman on board or getting a good night's sleep before each race. If you miss any of these you still don't have a valid reason for losing – they're all excuses which you're allowing to run you.

Your boat is probably your biggest superstition. It's simply a tool of racing, yet many sailors' egos are tied up with how shiny it is, or how many control lines run to each side deck. It's a perfectly reasonable goal to enjoy sailing in a boat that always looks like a highly polished piano, but you will then have to be content with your position in the race. Other people will have goals more in line with winning, and the chances are they'll beat you.

Boredom

It is often said that when learning stops, boredom begins. Sailing is a sport for life: that means some people will be racing for sixty years. Inevitably there are going to be periods when you feel you're in a rut. If you are bored with your racing, or you are no longer improving, take a look at it and take responsibility for it. Who is boring you? You're boring yourself.

Anyone who is committed and concentrating can't be bored. Apply some drills, do things, feel things, get your mind out of neutral. You might try the buddy system, and team up with another boat. In practice you can sail alongside each other, with one boat keeping everything constant while the other experiments by changing one variable at a time. Then swap over, to give the other boat a chance to make adjustments. On race day you can tune up with each other before the start, discuss the strategy for the day, even split tacks up a practice beat to see which side pays. If all that doesn't give you an interest (and make you a friend), try another buddy.

The killer instinct

Have you ever talked to the Club Mouse? His view goes like this: 'I don't win because I don't have the killer instinct. Actually I don't like doing anyone down, especially in a sport that is supposed to be fun.' In fact, if you are fully committed to doing your best, 'killing' other people does not come into it. When researching for his recent book *Sporting Excellence* British track star David Hemery interviewed 63 of sport's highest achievers, and the large majority never used or even advocated aggressive tactics. Such things are the cheap resort of the second-rate performer, afflicted by self-doubt.

Cheating

I am writing for those who seek to race within the rules, who wish for no unfair advantage, nor disadvantage. If you really have to cheat I don't have much to say to you save to ask 'Who are you really cheating, yourself or others?' If you win by unfair means, what have you proved? Most of us have probably considered cheating just a little at some time or other so I am not saying you are wrong for having had such thoughts. Just be aware of any temptation to cheat as it arises and if you act on it, at least face up to the possible consequences of your actions.

9   Getting a crew together

Although roll tacking, spinnaker drill and tactics are important, you won't get far unless you and your crew have common objectives. How you achieve those goals can be ironed out later; in the meantime everyone's intentions, desires and wishes need to be put on the table.

Even if you discover you have conflicting objectives, all is not lost. One of you might agree to drop his objective for a year, when the situation can be reviewed again.

Below: Common goals make a tight crew.

Before you start racing seriously both you and your potential crew will need to answer a whole range of questions:
- Do we have similar objectives?
- Are our skills complementary?
- Can we get on socially?
- Are we the right weight and shape for the boat?
- How much time can we invest?
- What are our differences in approach?

Why not try the awareness exercise on the following page? By the time you have spent an hour or so on it you will probably know

Qualities of a crew

Both of you write down, independently, five important qualities a crew should have. For example, here is one helmsman's list:

1. Co-operative
2. Strong
3. Supportive
4. Cheerful
5. Handy with tools

And here's his crew's list:

1. Correct height
2. Correct weight
3. Competitive attitude
4. Helming experience
5. Plenty of free time

Three of the qualities on the helmsman's list – but only one of his crew's – are internal ones and it is these that we are really looking for here. I suggest you each write two lists, one of the external and one of internal qualities. Here is my internal list:

1. Co-operation
2. Communication
3. Trust
4. Humour
5. Commitment

Now for the interesting part:

- Rate yourselves as a team (on a 0 to 10 scale) for each of the ten qualities on both of your lists, and have your partner do the same.
- Rate each of yourselves individually on all the qualities.
- Take each item in turn and explain to each other how you came to the rating that you gave.
- Now each of you say what you could do to up your rating to ten, on each of the items. Be specific: merely saying 'Communicate better' is not much use because it won't happen. 'In our next practice I'll tell you each time that. . .' is something you can both make sure happens.
- Tell each other what you each think the other could do to up the rating of each item, but do so in a constructive rather than accusing way.

more about each other than you would have gleaned from months of bar-side reminiscing. Just doing the exercise is bound to produce greater alignment. It is worth repeating the process a few times during the season. I guarantee your ratings will improve – along with your results. Perhaps your list of qualities will change too. Let them.

If you feel you don't know your crew well enough to do an exercise like this, you shouldn't be racing together. Sailing effectively is a far more complex business than answering a few questions.

Having done a little exercise to raise your awareness, let's get back to those six key questions I listed earlier.

1. Do we have similar objectives?

We're talking here about long-term objectives, such as winning a championship.

You need first to define your goal, then look at your respective levels of commitment to it. You should be willing to talk for hours about this. If you find you have different objectives *don't gloss over the fact*. Be honest with each other about your doubts about each other, and bear in mind that it's impossible to *persuade* someone to change an objective. Simply talking about your differences may well lead to alignment, or at least to someone suspending his or her objective till later.

Often you will not have seen the person clearly; you may have heard that he is difficult to sail with, projected that image onto him, then disliked the way he behaves. He may in fact be a joy to sail with provided he can find a helmsman as committed as he is himself.

2. Are our skills complementary?

A slightly modified version of the awareness exercise might help here. List the things you're good at, then the things you're bad at. Rate yourself out of ten on each, then get your crew to rate you. Meanwhile he can be drawing up his own list, and you can rate *him* on *it*.

Lots can come of this. For one thing, it is important for you to evaluate your own skills. Furthermore, by comparing scores you may find that the image you project is quite different: 'You gave me a 9 for spinnaker work but I only gave myself a 6 – why do you think I'm so good?' Provided you have good communication there need be no charge in this. And by acknowledging your weakness, the other person is far more likely to help.

If your friend is a little unsure of his spinnaker handling, perhaps you could give him a hand to set up the sheet and guy. If you have a tendency to throw away the start because you get neurotic, perhaps he can help you to focus your attention and to calm down at critical moments. In any case, if someone has admitted he's bad at, say, spotting windshifts it comes as no surprise later when he doesn't spot them. And no blame can be thrown, either.

Sometimes you find that somebody is good at one thing, but wants to do another. If the crew has a desire to do the tuning, let him do it! 'OK, while I'm on boatspeed you tweak the rig. We'll try that in the next practice session and for the first race, and monitor it carefully. But let's agree now to change the arrangement after the race if need be.' Either he'll become good at tuning, or he'll find he hasn't a clue and will stop the stream of 'helpful' suggestions. Whatever happens the boat will gain.

3. Can we get on socially?

Are you going to share a room on the circuit for cheapness? Are you going to drink in the evenings at regattas? Different people have different viewpoints. None is right or wrong; the important thing is that your views are aired.

Being irritated by someone's personal habits is going to get in the way, both socially and when you're sailing. You can either say something (which gives him the option of changing the habit) or learn to accept his habits for the sake of getting the best crewman going. That choice is yours. Either way, be clear about your choice and don't simply say nothing and fume. But if you are going to discuss the matter, first put yourself in his shoes. In what way would *you* like to be told about your pet mannerism? That's probably the best way to tell *him*.

4. Are we the right shape and weight for the boat?

You're unlikely to be successful in a Finn if you weigh 140lbs, or do well as a crew in a 470 if you weigh 200lbs. So either find a boat you can sail well together, or find a crew who fits your boat.

Motivation

One of the main differences between crew members is a mis-match in motivation:

- Rate yourselves, on a scale of 1-10, according to how much you can want to win. This at least makes you aware of how motivated you are.
- If you are low on motivation raise your awareness of what is stopping you being motivated.
- Now look at what can be done to raise the motivation of the least keen person. How does he feel about not being motivated? What about his responsibility to the rest of the crew? Will he agree *For a limited period* to up his keenness? ('How about giving us 10/10 for two hours?')
- Finally, agree to be open and honest with each other. If anyone becomes annoyed about something half-way through the race, he's got to be able to say it and the other has got to be prepared to listen without going through the roof.

In this way you can go through the season clearing up problems as they arise. The alternative is to drop into a pattern of bottled up energy and resentment which is both hard to break and a massive waste of energy.

5. How much time can we invest?

Obviously you need general agreement on the amount of time you plan to spend training, working on the boat and racing. Some aspects will be more important to one person; if you want the boat immaculate, make it your job and release your crew from feeling guilty about it. He can reciprocate by being responsible for something else.

6. What are our differences in approach?

How many boats have you seen with tense, tight-lipped crew? Each person is completely fed up with the other, but often the reason has not even been discussed, let alone resulted in an agreement.

Before things get to this stage, go sailing with the objective of finding all the differences you have in approach. Air the problems, and make agreements that you can both live with. Once an agreement is made, keep to it.

It is vital that you make an agreement you can keep – if you don't really mean to stick to it, if you don't recognise its value, if you're only saying yes because it says you should in this nice book, forget it.

If you can agree you will be a much happier crew. If you've both ageed that one of you is going to be boss today for example, and that person makes a wrong decision, the responsibility is shared.

I'm very hopeful that you will be able to build a good relationship in (and even out of) the boat. But what if it doesn't work?

If you established an honest relationship right at the beginning (and discussed the possibility of breaking up), then dissolving the partnership shouldn't be too much to bear. You could give yourselves six more races, and then re-evaluate the situation, but there's certainly no point in going on with something that doesn't work.

Yacht crews

Much of the foregoing applies equally well to the large crews of big boats. However, with more people in the crew there are obviously a number of additional factors to consider, and it is not my purpose to go into them all here. It could indeed be the subject of a whole book. I will nevertheless briefly describe one theory of group dynamics that I feel is especially appropriate to large yacht crews.

When any group is being formed, be it a nation, a business, a community or a sports team, it will display certain characteristics that can be divided into three distinct stages. The shift from one stage to the next is not sudden or clearly defined and, unfortunately, the third stage is a relatively rare occurence unless the group has been willing to use specific psycho-therapeutic techniques to achieve that stage. The benefits of reaching it are beyond anything one might expect but I doubt if many readers will know of a sailing crew who have achieved it.

Above: Even a high-performance craft is only as good as its crew.

The first stage is called *inclusion* . This is the time during which the predominant question in the crew member's mind is 'Do I belong here?' or 'Do I feel included?' Crew members will be a little withdrawn and tentative. This is in contrast to the second stage, known as the *control* stage in which many members' behaviour will be distinctly assertive. It is the stage in which the pecking order is established. Each member is looking to see where he fits, but is also flexing his muscles to establish his power in the group. Inevitably there is a certain amount of interpersonal competitiveness within the crew which wastes much of the energy and attention which would otherwise be spent on getting the job done.

This is, I suggest, where most crews are most of the time. Only rarely do crews achieve the third stage which is the *co-operation* stage. If they do reach it the crew

Inclusion stage

Each potential crew member should take the time to answer, honestly and thoughtfully, the following questions. It would be best if the crew members could pair off and ask each other the questions in turn. The effectiveness of the exercise depends on the willingness of the asker, or coach, to simply ask and listen, and ask again if anything is unclear, with no discussion or advice. Coaching one another in this way will give the crew members valuable insight into how they can help one another.

- Is this the boat I wish to crew on?
- Do I feel at home with these people?
- Do I complement this crew?
- How would I feel if I was rejected?
- What other boats could I crew on?
- What would that be like?
- Am I here now out of need or want?
- Can I imagine staying with this crew?

Make up more questions of your own as you proceed.

members voluntarily set aside their individual agendas to co-operate in achieving a common goal. The weaker members are supported when they fail, rather than rubbished which is what happens in the control stage. Trust between members is very high and a genuine affection between them develops. The focused attention of such a crew towards a clearly specified objective, such as a race, a championship or even the America's Cup, is fairly unbeatable.

It is a pity that, in spite of the vast amounts of money some people are willing to pour into the boats and latest equipment at this level of sailing, they rarely recognise the value of getting a well-matched crew together.

Control stage

Each crew member should print his or her name in large letters on a postcard. You then sit around a table with the cards face up, and arrange them in a line which represents the pecking order of the boat – with the most powerful person at one end and the mouse at the other. Each person is responsible for where he puts his own card, and for how he deals with the situation when someone else bumps him up or down. Find an order that everyone could live with.

The result, in fact, has little significance, but in the process of reaching it a number of hidden feelings will be expressed, usually in a playful harmless way, and the crew's covert power struggle will be dissipated. At the end discuss how you came to end up where you did and how you felt about it during the process, and how you feel about yourself now.

Co-operation stage

The awareness exercise at the beginning of this chapter is particularly helpful for building co-operation. Here are some more techniques:

- Switch functions with someone else on the boat and coach, rather than criticise, him into doing it well while he does the same for you.
- Set up a buddy system so that each person has a buddy with whom he agrees to share any concerns about himself, the crew or the boat. When a problem arises, they can decide together to deal with it fully and cleanly internally, or to bring it to the attention of the rest of the crew.
- Agree to hold regular crew meetings at which each person has three minutes without interruption to say what they like and dislike about the way the boat is running. The likes and appreciations are very important.
- This simple imagery exercise can be done alone or together. Sit comfortably, relax and breathe deeply for a few moments, then begin to imagine how a perfectly co-operative crew would behave. How would they interact? What qualities would they display? How would they cope with adversity? Give particular attention to how you would fit into this image. After a few minutes of this, imagine what specific steps your crew could take towards becoming perfectly co-operative. What steps could you personally take? Finally make the decision to take some of these steps – and do so at the earliest opportunity.

It is not difficult, though to do it thoroughly would demand the willingness of the crew to participate with sincerity, and the services of an experienced facilitator. Since such people are not usually to be found at the bar of the yacht club, try applying the techniques described in the shaded sections of this chapter.

The imagery exercise for co-operation delves a little way into the wisdom of your subconscious mind – your intuition. This is an invaluable resource which we rarely use, or even experience other than as an occasional spontaneous hunch. By being willing to set aside a little time – and suspending the mental chatter – the intuition can be evoked more or less to order. You will never know its value if you don't try it. If it does provide some useful answers for you, and it will, there is no limit to the other sailing and life situations to which you might apply this simple technique.

Each of the techniques described in this crew section demonstrate how you can become your own teacher if you trust that we all have a wellspring of inner wisdom. This art of self-coaching can be applied to evoke positive qualities or to eliminate negative ones in all the circumstances described throughout this book. You will have noticed that they all boil down to ways of raising your awareness of two vital questions: 'What is happening?' and 'What do I want?' The final chapter on goals deals more fully with 'What do I want?'

10 · Goals

Another logic would have placed the chapter on goals at the beginning of this book, but not mine. I regard goals as so important that I wanted you to be familiar with some of the mental principles previously discussed, as they will help you to understand the essential nature of goal setting.

You will have a much better chance of achieving a goal if you are able to define it accurately. 'I really want to be a success' is too general, because you could set off in so many different directions, but 'I really want to win the club Laser championship next year' is precise and the implication is clear: buy a fast boat and get your ass down to the sailing club.

Not only do you need to be clear about what you want, you've got to know how much you want it. It's a strange phenomenon that people who are 100 per cent committed to a realistic objective almost invariably achieve it, but a 95 per cent person (with 5 per cent of doubt) will have a success rate far lower than 95 per cent. If you doubt this, look back at the things you did not achieve and be honest with yourself about the degree of commitment you had, and then look at your commitment to those things that you did achieve.

Talking about his 1980 Olympic campaign, Ed Baird said:

'That was our most committed effort ever. We lived and breathed that Soling every day for a year, and in that time we came from nowhere, to rubbing shoulders with the top guys, to winning the US Nationals. I was so hyped that I won the Laser Worlds too, later that year. We had so much energy, nothing could stop us. If anything went wrong, that was fine – it was just a challenge to be overcome. We felt electric – we were flying.'

Although a precisely defined goal is paramount, there is no reason why you should not change your goal at any point as long as you are clear about your motivation for so doing. You might, for example, keep changing it until you find a goal you're 100 per cent committed to. It is the commitment that counts, not the goal. In fact the real purpose of having a goal is to evoke commitment, which is only possible if there is something specific and time-phased to go for. Open-ended goals are very hard to commit yourself to.

In 1965 I won the European Saloon Car Championship, something which the Ford Motor Company employed me to do. Twenty years on the cup lies dented and tarnished in the attic, and the photographs have lost their colour, but the experience of having put my guts into a long, hard and successful season still brings me a joyful nostalgia.

Many people think that the goal is all-important, and that to get there, you need to be committed, and so you do. However, when you discover that the fulfilment, the joy and the learning all come from the commitment and not the goal, the pot on the mantlepiece fades into insignificance – and you have a new goal.

1. So you do need to have a goal

Think carefully, then list all your goals as precisely as you can. Your first attempt might look something like this:

- To win the championship
- To do something else with my friends
- To have a good time down at the sailing club
- To find new friends
- To get away from the office claustrophobia into wide open spaces
- To be successful at something, anything

2. Clarify your goals

Which championship do you want to win? Do you want to win it this year, or next? Which friend have you in mind and is sailing together really what you both want to do? How many new friends?

3. Eliminate the fuzzy ones

Any goal that you are at all uncertain about, that you cannot make specific and time-phased, or that you feel *should* be a goal of yours but *really* you don't care about, should be crossed out. Fuzzy goals are not goals at all and will not help you with your commitment.

4. Eliminate any goal you've set to please other people

If you've listed any of these goals with the idea of impressing your nearest and dearest, or the world at large, cross it out. The only goal that will work is the one that is for you yourself; you won't get any satisfaction from others saying you did well if you know you didn't. Conversely, if you know you did as well as you could, it doesn't matter what anyone says. Ultimately you have to match up to your own criteria, or your satisfaction will depend on the whims of other people.

5. Are your goals realistic?

To be a success it is essential to set yourself achieveable goals, and eliminate any that are not. You can always reinstate them later as you progress, and as they become realistic. For example, this season you could aim at the Winter Series, but leave the Nationals to next year.

6. Do you really intend to do them?

Are you one of those people who always have a couple if items left on their *things to do* list at the end of the day? You know, the ones like 'take my jacket to the dry cleaners', 'Go to the car wash on the way home' or 'Phone about the insurance rebate'? Unsatisfying isn't it? How about never putting anything on the list that you do not fully intend to do? Any that have remained undone for more than four days may as well be crossed out.

Inevitably there is some disappointment attached to lowering your sights. But the sooner you get on with the goals you *are* going for, rather than worrying about the ones you've no hope of achieving, the better.

7. Rate each goal

Now rate the goals that are left on a scale of 1-10, and put them in order. If there is a clear ranking, fine. But if you have goals with equal ratings, or if they're contradictory in nature you clearly have to make a choice. 'I want to win the championships and drink with my friends every night' is a classic example. Sailors who can't make a choice usually stay up too late to win next day, but not late enough to really enjoy themselves.

If you really can't decide where your priorities lie, flip a coin and then really go for it. If it doesn't work out, you probably picked the wrong objective, and you're now clear which one you really do want.

Sometimes you can resolve conflicting goals by scheduling them. 'OK, for the next month let's sail every day and win the championship. After that, let's do some regattas, and have fun.' The only decision most human beings make is to be indecisive. Are you going to be one of them?

8. Find your commitment level

Finally look at your number one goal. Let's suppose it's winning a championship. What is your percentage commitment? You can find this out by asking what you'd give up to achieve it. Would you give up your job? Would you work nights to buy new sails? Really, truly, how much do you want to win?

Note that there's nothing wrong with having only 90 per cent commitment to winning, but if you feel that way don't expect to win too much. Can you find 100 per cent commitment? It might be better to change your goal to something you *are* committed to 100 per cent then do it. In this case it might be finishing in the first three while still keeping a full-time job, that is, a modified version of your number one goal. Or it might be that you choose to go full tilt for your number two or number three goals, or a combination of numbers one and two. Ultimately what goals you choose matters less than the level of commitment you can generate. As I have stressed already the thrill, the joy, the performance, the learning, the pleasure and the satisfaction we all seek through our sporting activities does not come from achieving the goal or even from the sailing itself. It comes from the commitment. You could sail and even win a few cups without experiencing any of those things. But by experiencing total commitment – in sailing – you will know the complete fulfilment that is available to you in any field you choose – if you do it with as much commitment.

What are the obstacles to achieving your goals?

- In two columns, under the headings External and Internal, list all the things you think are standing in your way, leaving a space in the Internal column opposite each of your external obstacles.
- In this space insert the internal component of the external obstacle. For example, you may have 'Lack of money' in your External column; what might appear opposite it would be 'My belief that my old boat is not as fast as the others' or 'My unwillingness to work harder or get a better-paid job'.
- In your External column you now have a list of obstacles, some of which may seem to be outside your control. However, the corresponding items in the Internal column bring all of these problems within your control. By accepting responsibility you empower yourself. Note that I am not denying the external reasons (no one wants to sail a slow boat), but your internal reaction to them will hinder you more. So let go of those external things you really cannot do anything about and concentrate on the things you *can* do something about, the internal components.
- If you have trouble identifying the obstacles, adopt the 'What, When, Where, How much' technique that we used before for internal obstacles to performance.

What is my interference?
When does it occur?
Where does it occur?
How much (on a scale of 1-10) does it interfere?

This should clarify your awareness of your obstacles. 'My anxiety about boatspeed is my interference. I only worry about it on the first lap, and mainly on the first beat. It wrecks me 5/10 on the Richter scale.'

- There are numerous destructive tendencies which are also obstacles. You should be able to find several of these but to give you an idea of the kind of things to identify, and to jog your memory, here are four obstacles which are very common in sailing.

One is to blame poor speed on the boat. I'm sorry to tell you that 90 per cent of the time it's you, not the rig or hull. If you don't believe me, get someone you admire to sail your boat. Usually you'll be amazed how fast she goes.

Another mental obstacle is the assumption that the big names are always faster than you. Quite often they are not, but what they are is much more

Why sail?

In conclusion, and appropriately in the chapter on goals, I want to come back again to the question of why do you sail? Some of you may answer that you live for your sailing, which implies that life is not worth much when you are not sailing – which is probably most of the time. Life is only that stuff you use to fill in the spaces between sailing. Of course you have to earn the money to enable you to sail so maybe you can see your job in a positive light, as the provider of sailing. However if you could earn as much by doing something else for less time, you probably would, and where does it all leave your home life?

I lived for motor racing, for a while. I was very committed, very successful, and very consistent. Check out their championship results: hardly ever does anyone win every race. And anyway, speed isn't the only thing. In fact, speed in the wrong direction puts you even further back! In sailing everyone has a chance.

A third is the inability to resist doing something desperate, or at the very least inappropriate to catch up with the leaders. If they are sailing well, you have to settle for the waiting game and just keep sailing at your best. Often they will make a mistake or two which may give you a chance. If they don't, there is nothing you can do anyway.

A fourth is the fear of success. Some people fear winning because of forebodings about what it may lead to. 'If I win the club championship I'll have to go round all the open meetings' or 'I'll have to give up all those hard luck stories which get me so much sympathy and attention'. I have to admit that I am short on compassion for this problem. It sounds like the ultimate 'Poor me'. In fact, if you win the club championship you don't have to do anything. You can retire if you like, and take up golf.

• To eliminate each obstacle may not require great struggle and effort. Accurately identifying it is half the battle. A major advantage of the internal approach to problem solving is that awareness itself is inherently curative. We are dominated by the obstacles that we are unaware of. We gain control over things of which we are fully conscious. In other words, once a problem is highlighted, it soon ceases to be a problem.

• Take responsibility for the internal obstacles to your goals, and for the obstacles that arise on the day. As I have already emphasised, the internal approach obliges us to be responsible for ourselves and our actions and thereby empowers us. Let's look at another example to illustrate the point more graphically. Suppose you are going pretty slowly and you reckon the sails are wrong. Your conclusion is that the boat can't win with this rig. You sit back, playing 'poor me'. How could the sailmaker have done this to me! But wait a minute. Who bought those sails? Who hoisted them today? Who is forcing you to use them? and in any case, if Paul Elvstrom were using them, would he be back here? How bad are they really? And what about tactics and strategy? Can't you get up there without raw speed? Wouldn't a better approach be to decide to change the sails when the race is over, and in the meantime put them out of your mind and get on with the race. Again, with responsibility comes the power to change things.

blinkered. I would not have missed it for the world, and though I did not know it at the time, it has provided me with many important lessons and benefits for my life since. I started racing as the timid son of a benevolent and successful but autocratic father in whose shadow I hid my mediocrity during my school years. Racing took me out into the world, taught me self-responsibility, gave me self-esteem and helped me to come to terms with despair and triumph, fear and joy, life and death. I enjoyed those years like no others. In the exact science of hindsight I realise now that while I lived for racing I was more importantly racing for my life. Though I had had a taste before, it was not until I made this realisation that I was able to

Intermediate goals: the willingness to drop or change them

If your ultimate goal is to win a championship, do you necessarily need to win today's club race? It might well be better to treat it as a training sesssion. For example, suppose you're weak in light winds and today's little race is in Force 1. As predicted the club light-weather ace leaves you miles behind on the first lap. Why not forget the result and use the race as a practice? Slow down, let him lap you, then follow him. Copy his jib lead positions, see how tight his vang is, note how his boat is trimmed. Can you set your boat up the same way and keep up with him? What could you have learned from a mile astern anyway?

Of suppose you've made a disastrous start because you capsized at the critical moment. What are you going to do? Shout and curse? or learn? You could have a great time just trying to overtake one boat, or practise sailing the boat *exactly* upright for the whole beat (and see what happens) or try raking the mast back/forward from normal and assessing the speed. Whatever you do is bound to be more fun than tagging along behind, hating every minute of it. And you might just stumble on something you can use in the future.

One of my most enjoyable and memorable races was when I was driving in the Tourist Trophy for jazz trombonist Chris Barber whose car, on this occasion, was very poorly prepared. It soon became obvious to me that I had no chance of winning my class. For some reason I did not get depressed; I accepted the situation and then I had nothing to lose. I changed my goal. I decided to spend the afernoon getting the car right. I pulled into the pits again and again and gradually got the engine, the suspension and the handling balance set up as I liked it. Then during the last hour of the race I managed to lap faster than the class leaders and really enjoyed myself. It was one of the best races I ever drove, and I finished last!

fully harvest the fruits of my experiences. How much richer and more beneficial would my racing have been if I had known why I was really doing it? I cannot be sure, but I retired twenty years ago and have had a rich and fulfilling life since.

You may sail well into your seventies, so I hope you don't have to wait until your retirement to harvest the fruits of your sailing. I recommend that you start now to view your sailing as a school for the rest of your life. If you do so, losing a championship will be almost as good as winning it, and making a total hash of the start of the race you should have won will be as amusing to you as it is to the rest of the club. You will be able to reap the benefits of non-attachment and dis-identification from the results of your sailing. You will have the freedom to learn, to enjoy and to perform without the encumbrance of your anxious mind. You will be able to become the natural, free, sensitive champion sailor that is within your potential. You will, truly, be sailing for your life.

Go for it!

Other books in the Sail to Win series

Tactics *Rodney Pattisson*
A guide to boat-to-boat tactics and strategy around an Olympic course, by gold medallist Rodney Pattisson.

Dinghy Helming *Lawrie Smith*
One of Britain's top helmsmen gives specific advice on maximising boatspeed in all conditions, plus helming skills required during the race itself.

Dinghy Crewing *Julian Brooke-Houghton*
Crewing a modern racing dinghy is a complex and demanding task. Olympic medallist Julian Brooke-Houghton explains the skills required and shows how helmsman and crew work together as a race-winning team.

Wind Strategy *David Houghton*
Most 'sailing weather' books are too large-scale to be relevant to racing on inland or coastal waters. This book shows how to predict the wind over the racecourse area, during the time-span of the race, using simple 'rules of thumb'.

Tuning Your Dinghy *Lawrie Smith*
A logical, systematic approach to setting up a racing dinghy and fine-tuning it on all points of sailing. Plus a 'trouble shooting' section to pinpoint and cure specific weaknesses in the boat's performance.

The Rules in Practice *Bryan Willis*
It is a popular fallacy among racing sailors that you need to know the rules. You *do* need to know your rights and obligations on the water – the rules can always be looked up afterwards. International rules experts Bryan Willis looks at the key situations that repeatedly occur on championship courses, from the viewpoint of each helmsman in turn, and summarises what you may, must or cannot do.

Tides and Currents *David Arnold*
How tides can help you win races – whether inshore, offshore or on an Olympic triangle.

Boatspeed – Supercharging your hull, foils and gear *Rodney Pattison*
Written by an Olympic Gold Medallist, this book gives the secrets of achieving a really fast boat – whether new or second-hand – plus detailed information on choosing and installing all the control systems.

Sails *John Heyes*
It's impossible to be a good sailor without a knowledge of sails. This complete guide shows how they work, how to buy them, how to set them and what can be done to improve them.

Also published by Fernhurst Books

Sailing the Mirror *Roy Partridge*
Topper Sailing *John Caig*
The Laser Book *Tim Davison*
Laser Racing *Ed Baird*
Yacht Crewing *Malcolm McKeag*
Yacht Skipper *Robin Aisher*
Boardsailing: a beginner's manual *John Heath*
Board Racing *Geoff Turner & Tim Davison*
Dee Caldwell's Book of Freestyle Boardsailing *Dee Caldwell*
Must I go down to the sea again? *Lesley Black/illustrated by Mike Peyton*
Knots & Splices *Jeff Toghill*

SAIL TO WIN

THE BOOK ... Ninety per cent of winning takes place from the neck up, yet most books concentrate on gear and technique. The real opposition, located somewhere inside the sailor's head. *The Winning Mind* looks at This book shows how mental attitude affects your enjoyment and your racing success. It gives practical exercises to help both helmsman and crew relax, become more efficient, concentrate better and sail faster. If your sailing is boring, if your crew is demotivated or if you feel psyched out, this book is the tonic you need.

THE AUTHOR ... As a professional racing driver, John Whitmore needed a relaxed mind free of anxiety. This led to his studying psychology and its application in sport. He now teaches amateurs and professionals to master the mental side of a wide variety of sports.

THE SERIES ... *The Winning Mind* is part of the Sail to Win series – books by world class sailors and coaches which take a fresh look at the complex subject of racing. Each book gives the detailed expert advice that the competent sailor must have to overcome the "club racer" barrier and compete successfully in international fleets. The emphasis is on practical, effective information presented in a straightforward manner.

Fernhurst Books

ISBN 0-906754-30-5

9 780906 754306